W9-CNF-693

United Nations Office at Vienna
Centre for Social Development and Humanitarian Affairs

THE IMPACT OF ECONOMIC AND POLITICAL REFORM ON THE STATUS OF WOMEN IN EASTERN EUROPE

Proceedings of a United Nations Regional Seminar

Vienna, 8-12 April 1991

UNITED NATIONS
New York, 1992

NOTE

Symbols of United Nations documents are composed of capital letters combined with figures. Mention of such a symbol indicates a reference to a United Nations document.

The designations employed and the presentation of the material in this publication do not imply the expression of any opinion whatsoever on the part of the Secretariat of the United Nations concerning the legal status of any country, territory, city or area or of its authorities, or concerning the delimitation of its frontiers or boundaries.

ST/CSDHA/19

UNITED NATIONS PUBLICATION

Sales No.: E.92.IV.4

ISBN 92-1-130152-1

Foreword

The Regional Seminar on the Impact of Economic and Political Reform on the Status of Women in Eastern Europe and the Union of Soviet Socialist Republics: The Role of National Machinery took place at Vienna from 8 to 12 April 1991. It was the first time that the role of women in the changes occurring in the region had been discussed at the level of the United Nations. It reflected the belief that if appropriate attention was given to that role, the reform process could be made smoother and more effective.

The Seminar brought together women and men with distinct experiences and points of view. Some were officials of national governmental institutions concerned with the advancement of women. Others were members of non-governmental organizations. Still others were scholars who had begun to examine the reform process. Among the observers were representatives of Governments and international organizations. Over the five days, there were full and frank discussions. But the overall atmosphere was optimistic and, despite differences on many issues, the participants worked in a cooperative way.

The papers presented by the participants and the results of the discussion constitute an early examination of the reform process and the problems that need to be addressed.* They were prepared by the participants in their individual capacity. The Seminar itself was organized at short notice and the papers had to be prepared with little time for reflection and careful drafting. They reflect the information available to the authors, their passion and concern, and their own style of presenting ideas.

Because of the importance of the changes occurring in the region and the need to provide information from the perspective of women, the proceedings of the Seminar are being published. In so doing, an effort has been made to condense the original papers and present them in a consistent style.

The Seminar itself was largely funded by the United Nations Development Programme (UNDP) as part of its regional programme. UNDP was joined by the Governments of Sweden and the United States of America in providing extrabudgetary resources, without which the Seminar could not have been held. The Government of Sweden provided additional resources that permitted the publication of the proceedings of the Seminar.

The result demonstrates once again that successful development and productive and peaceful change requires the full and active participation of women.

Chafika Meslem
Director
Division for the Advancement of Women
Centre for Social Development and Humanitarian Affairs
United Nations Office at Vienna

---

* It should be noted that all the papers in this publication were published before April 1991. Therefore, the names of the countries concerned are those that were in use prior to that date.

CONTENTS

INTRODUCTION

The Seminar had a number of objectives. First, to make a clear and convincing identification of the gender factors involved in a reform process, and what might be called "the woman dimension" in economic and political changes. Also, to identify the challenges and opportunities for women in this critical and exciting process.

Secondly, to identify steps that Governments, enterprises, groups and individuals could take to ensure that the full force of "woman power" can be applied in the individual countries of Eastern Europe and to produce concrete and realistic recommendations that could be applied to national situations.

Thirdly, to identify innovative forms of international cooperation that could extend assistance across national and regional boundaries, which should lead to suggestions on how the issue of women could be mainstreamed in the overall assistance being provided both from private and public sources to the countries of Eastern Europe.

Finally, although it would be difficult to measure, it was hoped that the Seminar could result in the kind of networking of personal relations between individuals of different countries in a common cause that could, over the medium-term, provide new opportunities for mutual support.

It must also be taken as given that in most countries in Eastern Europe today the reform process is considered to be gender-neutral. This reflects in some measure a certain success over the past decades in Eastern Europe: equality between the sexes has been enshrined in law, women have achieved equal rates of participation in the labour force, and women have had equal access to basic education and social services. On this basis it could be assumed by policy makers that reform affects women and men alike.

That assumption, however, masks a latent inequality that existed before the reform process began. It is a fact that women tended to be employed in the lower paid sectors of the economy, were not able to benefit equally from training and technological innovation and did not have equivalent career paths. They were required, more than men, to maintain the household even while working and, although formally represented in parliaments, were notably absent at the levels where real political and economic decisions were made, whether for the State or for the enterprise.

A characteristic of the reforms is the transition from a command economy to a market economy. This involves an emphasis on entrepreneurship and the management style that accompanies it. The greatest areas of growth in the economy are likely to be in small to medium-sized enterprises producing goods that were not produced before, or producing them in different ways for different markets. The management style required for this new economy is based on a careful relationship of productive resources to output, careful management of their use, attention to the needs of the consumers for whom the goods are produced and attention to the concerns of the workers whose productivity will determine the profit margins of the firm.

By not having been involved in the management of the command economy, women may not have acquired the particular management habits that went with that economy. Indeed, women constitute a new pool from which new managers can be drawn. In managing their households and providing for their families in periods of scarcity over the past years, women of Eastern Europe have had to behave very much like the kind of managers which the transition to the market economy will require. Much more than men, women in Eastern Europe and the USSR are already entrepreneurs.

The potential of women to take their existing, if unrecognized, management skills and apply them in the new and growing areas of economy in Eastern Europe and the USSR is illustrated by the recent historical experience of some Western industrialized countries in which women make up a very high percentage of the owners and managers of small and medium-sized enterprises.

Whether this potential can be unleashed, however, will depend on a combination of public policy and private opportunities. First, women must be made aware of their potential to be major economic actors. Secondly, the necessary financial and technological resources, including training, must be made available to them. And thirdly, the women entering this part of the economy must help each other.

A further question is how to be assure that public policies will be directed to this end and that women will become conscious of their potential. There were two important issues in this respect.

The first is the role of national machinery for the advancement of women. Without a strong national machinery mobilizing information on women and making it available to both policy makers and to women themselves, it is unlikely that gender aspects of the reform process can be convincingly advocated. As in other regions, national machinery for the advancement of women is often under-financed, not well connected to policy making and lacks the necessary networking with scholars, women's organizations and the international system that would be necessary for success.

It is desirable to examine how national machinery in Eastern Europe could be strengthened.

Secondly, women's issues must be addressed by women themselves. Unless women perceive their interests and act on them in the political as well as in the economic sphere, there is little likelihood that public policy will respond to women's concerns. Perhaps this is best reflected in the fact that although women constitute half of the electors in all Eastern European countries, the percentage of women elected to parliament is well below European averages - primarily because women are not selected as candidates. But women are not selected as candidates because the political leaders of the parties concerned do not believe that this has any bearing on their party's success. Women must convince them of the contrary.

Low priority for women's concerns in the political process is encouraged by the absence of strong women's organizations, representing a diversity of interests and positions, who could come together in support of wider issues. How to develop these organizations should be a concern.

Advancement of women is an issue that not only transcends national boundaries but in which the co-operation and the pressure for advancement of women mounted at the international level provides a powerful weapon for women within countries where they lack equal access to decision-making. International instruments such as the Convention on the Elimination of All Forms of Discrimination against Women, to which almost all countries of Eastern Europe and the USSR are parties, and the Nairobi Forward-looking Strategies,[1] to which they have all subscribed, provide standards women can use in judging their own countries.

These instruments should be used, and they must be publicized among women of the region.

The new developments in the region have stimulated considerable interest in international co-operation to support the reform process. The pace of reform will be influenced by the kind of international cooperation - both technical and financial - that will be received. The question is how this cooperation can be oriented so as to ensure that it reaches and involves women. It is, perhaps, another indication of the universality of development questions that this is the same question of mainstreaming that is considered in other regions, and the tools applied can be the same. The main instrument is to ensure that gender analysis is made whenever a loan, a project or an agreement is proposed. This analysis ideally should be made jointly by the recipient country and by the donor.

The transition to a market economy places emphasis on the cooperating role of the private sector. This is worked out in joint ventures, in production, in investment and in the transfer of technology and skills. In many of the fields in which growth is likely to occur in Eastern Europe, it is women entrepreneurs who could provide both examples of sources of partnerships. Similarly, the training of women entrepreneurs in Western industrialized countries is often most effectively carried out by associations of these entrepreneurs themselves.

Finally, it is important to underscore the important role international non-governmental organizations can play in identifying, encouraging and supporting women in Eastern Europe, both by supporting existing organizations and encouraging the development of new ones. How this can best be done is a worthwhile question.

---

[1] Report of the World Conference to Review and Appraise the Achievements of the United Nations Decade for Women: Equality, Development and Peace, Nairobi, Kenya, 15-26 July 1985 (United Nations publication, Sales No. E.85.IV.10), chap. I, sect. A.

Part One: Working Papers

I. WOMEN'S ROLE IN MAKING REFORM WORK*

The process of political and economic reform in Eastern Europe and the USSR constitutes an opportunity to improve the status of women in those countries, but it also threatens to retard progress. Moreover, mobilizing the latent capabilities of women can become a major factor in achieving success in the reforms. Whether this occurs will depend on the extent to which public policies and private actions take into account gender-related factors, whether women themselves become active in the process and the extent to which international cooperation occurs.

In terms of the economy, reform is based generally on the replacement of centralized forms of directive planning with market-oriented policies and structures. While the timing, character, phasing and impact of these reforms has varied countries, some common features are as follows:

(a) Redistribution of economic power from State planning and administration to private and cooperative enterprises;

(b) Incorporation and strengthening of market mechanisms;

(c) Institution of market-oriented fiscal and monetary policy;

(d) Movement towards private and cooperative ownership rather than State and collective ownership;

(e) Increased use of material benefits and wage/salary differentials in order to improve productivity;

(f) Greater integration with the international economy.

The reform process also involves changes in the legislative and political systems in order to ensure economic changes and to provide the appropriate mechanisms for the participation of people in decision-making in all spheres. This has included a relaxation of previous controls to allow greater freedom of expression and association, more cultural diversity, and ideological tolerance and greater openness to the rest of the world. It has also included provision for the comprehensive development of human rights.

Reform is not gender-neutral

The nature of reform in each country differs according to national conditions, both in terms of past development and present resources, and to priorities in economic and social spheres. However, a common factor is that the advancement of women is not considered a priority for the reform process or an important factor. There is an assumption that the reform process is gender-neutral.

It can be shown that there are significant differences for men and women in terms of the impact of the reform process and on the means to promote its success. How these issues are addressed during this critical and volatile transitional period can determine the long-term success of the reform.

Under the previous system, despite formal reports to the contrary, the advancement of women in Eastern European countries had some success, but did not lead to the elimination of women's subordinate position in society. As in other regions, the most important aspect of women's advancement was the legal provision for equal rights for men and women in

all spheres of life combined with the institutional measures to implement them. In addition to equal access of women to participate in the economy as well as equal access to education a situation was created that might have led to an assumption that women had gained de facto equality.

However, many negative effects have also accumulated that constitute a base of inequality upon which the reform processes are being built. These include a high concentration of women in the lower levels of professional and skill structures, low representation of women in decision-making bodies, especially at the higher levels of economic policy-making, and a continuation of an unequal division of labour in the family.

The intense involvement of women in the labour force that characterizes Eastern European countries has not been accompanied by changes in the division of labour in the family. To some extent, the goal of the emancipation of women by their participation in the paid labour force has been discredited by the

---

* by the Division for the Advancement of Women, United Nations Office at Vienna.

existence of a double burden on women. Indeed, in some countries, the fact that women have had to undertake responsibilities for taking care of the family in addition to their waged work has been used as a grounds for denying them the same career prospects as men (as being "unreliable workers") and contributes to the absence of women in management and at decision-making levels.

The concept of social protection is widespread in the Eastern European countries and is based on strong centralization and the primacy of the State over other elements of social structure, such as the individual, the family or the enterprise, who were not held to be completely competent to meet social needs. It was primarily the responsibility of the State to render assistance. A characteristic of this premise was that there was no place for personal autonomy or the free development of the individual. This, coupled with the traditional view of women as the weaker sex fulfilling the "natural" roles of wife and mother, led to considering assistance to women and improvement of their status as a form of protection, to which a number of sex-specific privileges were added.

It is largely because of the previous base of de facto inequality, masked by an apparent equality between the sexes in terms of law and gross statistics of economic participation and access to services, that the reform policies are not gender-neutral, even though they may appear so.

Economic reform implies intensification of production, changes in enterprise ownership patterns, managerial practices and, perhaps, shifts in the composition of the industrial base of the countries concerned.

Prior to restructuring, there was occupational segregation and concentration of employed women in particular industrial sectors. A large number of women were working in education and health care, public catering, insurance and banking. In general, women were involved in low-skilled, low-wage, labour-intensive sectors of the economy. It is these sectors, including government administration, that are most likely to be affected by economic restructuring leading to plant closures, sectoral readjustments and, accordingly, unemployment. At the same time support services for women workers, such as childcare facilities, are closing on the grounds that they are inefficient and cannot be provided by the new market-oriented employers or by the State.

There is a danger that the female labour force in Eastern European countries may be further marginalized in that they may find themselves on the periphery of major economic structures in the new economic environment and become concentrated in sectors characterized by low wages, low skill require-

ments, intermittent employment, a limited number of available occupations, bad working conditions, horizontal professional mobility and part-time employment. This in turn could lead to increased female poverty.

Economic reform has led to new forms of employment such as self-employment, work in the cooperatives and private enterprises. To the extent that women had, in the past, unequal access to economic and social resources, technology and markets and adequate management training, women now may not benefit from the new reforms.

Economic changes are guided by political decisions. In the political sphere, women have not been well-represented at the highest levels of decision-making, but have had considerable formal participation in parliaments. One consequence of giving parliaments a significant role in decision-making has been to decrease the representation of women. As a result of the elections held in 1990 in Bulgaria, the percentage of women in parliament fell from 21 to 8.5; in Czechoslovakia, from 29.5 to 6; in the German Democratic Republic, from 32.2 to 20.5; in Hungary, from 20.9 to 7; and in Romania, from 34.3 to 3.5.

Although the process of democratization, which is part of economic and political changes, has resulted in the emergence of new organizational forms, women have not played a major part in them. In addition, women's organizations are undergoing major reform as those formerly supported by the State have less influence and new, informal organizations have yet to develop.

Part of the reform process is the articulation of family values. This may be in reaction to the previous ideology, which emphasized collective societal values over individual and family. The issue is not the values themselves, since the family remains a critical aspect of human organization, but the way in which these values are expressed in terms of sex roles. If, as was traditionally the case, family roles are associated only with women, they can be used a a means of denying women the opportunity to participate fully in other spheres of life.

It should be noted that maintenance of an acceptable standard of living is based on two incomes in the family. There is thus a contradiction between the traditional perception of women as mothers and wives and their professional objectives. This is aggravated by the demographic situation in which national birth rates are at replacement level or lower. The negative correlation between level of fertility and labour force participation has led the supporters of traditional values to the view that women should return to child-bearing and rearing.

The extent to which women wish to accept such policies is not being examined at the policy-making level. Nor are possible policies that would permit reconciliation of family and work responsibilities of both sexes. The absence of women at decision-making levels who might articulate the opposite viewpoint aggravates the situation. This is also related to such issues as family-planning policy, the implementation of which would allow women to exercise their rights fully and would serve as protection of maternity and childhood.

A critical role for women in the reform process

Development is impossible without human resource development. The abandonment of this principle played a major role in the collapse of former systems in Eastern European countries, where there was little space for individual development. Human-resource development should be seen as more than education and health, and should extend beyond the concept of the human being as a generator of resources and a source of productivity. Mobilization of the latent capabilities of women in all spheres is an important aspect in the process of development.

Any tendency to explain economic development primarily in terms of capital and technology inputs ignores the fact that human beings and the skills they command are decisive for development and that investment in human capital can yield higher returns than financial capital formation. Comparative cost advantages increasingly accrue to products and services that are non-material.

New opportunities exist within the period of transformation to increase efforts in the professional training of women. Women already have a high level of education and thus the background and capability to adapt to change. They have a major contribution to make in ensuring the successful transition of these countries from centrally planned to market-oriented economies.

As technological innovations are supposed to be one of the essential macroeconomic dimensions of change, it is possible to assume that future developments in industry will lead to increased complexity of industrial technologies. Women should not be excluded from such technological innovations on the grounds of protection. On the contrary, their partici-pation in these processes should be ensured by appropriate education and training. Indeed, the transformation of traditional production processes by technological changes creates a basis for overcoming gender-based occupational segregation.

With the new emphasis on industrial innovations and entrepreneurship observed in Eastern European countries, it appears essential to ensure a stronger participation of women not only in the industrial labour force but also in entrepreneurial activities.

Women's potential to be entrepreneurs may not be well recognized. However, it can be argued that in their management of the household and work responsibilities, women already function as entrepreneurs. This activity is not recorded in statistics because such activities are either non-renumerated or regarded as a sideline. However, with proper training and access to capital and technology, they might form the core of a new class of entrepreneurs in Eastern European countries, just as has happened in Western industrialized countries. Moreover, the growth of female entrepreneurship coupled with the higher levels of industrial skills of women workers can provide a major stimulus for overall growth, generating increased employment opportunities and higher levels of income.

The changing economic and political environment in Eastern European countries has created new challenges and new opportunities for people to re-evaluate policies, practices and institutions, including the way in which men and women can best contribute to and benefit from economic and social development.

Incorporation of gender concerns in policy-making

It is important to begin to establish an institutional framework for human-resource planning, comprising both men and women, and to make it an integral part of economic and social policy-making. Gender-sensitive policy is interdisciplinary. Women's issues are linked to the structures, laws and attitudes in almost every sphere of life, education, employment, health care and the family. Many policy makers still have not realized this fact. But their political will is required to incorporate gender concerns into policy-making.

Policy formulation relies on adequate information, including statistics. Therefore, the development and maintenance of regular statistical series disaggregated by gender are essential.

Formulating demands is the task of women themselves through women's organizations, political parties and other institutions. The existence of informal women's movements of different types is of particular importance. The previous system left little room for such activity. Several generations of women were given to understand that discrimination did not exist and that there was no need to struggle actively for their rights. This partially explains the low level of consciousness among many women and their support for traditional approaches to women's issues.

Of considerable importance, therefore, is work aimed at increasing women's awareness of their existing rights, to better identify their needs and thus exert pressure in the political process to promote more favourable attitudes towards women and facilitate their participation in different spheres of life.

Adequate policies can be realized only when more women obtain decision-making positions. The demand for the equal participation of women in political decision-making is not only a question of democracy, but also prerequisite to women's interest being taken into account in policy-making.

National machinery for the advancement of women should be established. The type of structure may vary from country to country, but general principles might be formulated. An analysis undertaken by the United Nations suggests the following factors should be considered in establishing national machinery:

(a) Level within the governmental structure at which it is operating;

(b) Political support, authority and access to power;

(c) Available resources in terms of information, staff and finance;

(d) Ability to establish and maintain linkages with other governmental structures and non-governmental organizations.

In order to strengthen national machinery, a number of strategies could be considered, including:

(a) Wide use of existing international documents, including the Convention on the Elimination of All Forms of Discrimination against Women;

(b) Statement that the advancement of women should be governmental policy with defined short-term and long-term targets;

(c) Examination of proposed governmental policies and programmes in terms of their likely effects on the status of women;

(d) Regular exchange of information, and the establishment of information systems for monitoring developments;

(e) Organization of mass-media campaigns aimed at eliminating sexist stereotypes and attracting more public attention to issues of equality between men and women;

(f) Establishment of linkages with the scientific community and encouragement of institutions to conduct research on different aspects of women's status.

The greater use of market mechanisms, new forms of political organization of the State and increased integration into international economic relations suggest that these countries will confront some of the same opportunities and constraints as most other European countries. In order to be part of that new regional system, countries of Eastern Europe and the USSR should follow the strategies towards women's issues developed by the international community. The international community, in the form of such organizations as the European Communities (EC) and the Economic Commission for Europe (ECE) of the United Nations should make it clear that women's issues are among the important matters on their agenda and that in discussion of international cooperation the gender approach should be apparent.

Since Eastern European countries face a similar set of problems it might be reasonable to formulate outlines for regional policy, initiating projects and programmes especially for this transitional period. Consideration might be given to a role for the ECE in coordinating such activities, whether separately or as part of other activities. The contribution that could be made by other parts of the United Nations system should also be examined.

Women must decide their own future. They must call attention to shortcomings in policies and programmes, make recommendations for action, put pressure on their Governments and political parties, propose models for positive action, analyse proposed policies, disseminate information on a large scale and organize mass media campaigns. The idea of national strategies to incorporate women fully into the reform process might be explored, both internationally and by the countries concerned.

II. THE ROLE AND TASK OF NATIONAL MACHINERY FOR THE ADVANCEMENT OF WOMEN IN THE PERIOD OF SOCIAL AND ECONOMIC REFORM IN THE COUNTRIES OF EASTERN EUROPE AND THE USSR*

Introduction

Since the submission of reports to the United Nations on the implementation of the Convention on the Elimination of All Forms of Discrimination against Women by the countries of Eastern Europe, the region has undergone radical political and social transformations. To facilitate an understanding of the implications of these changes for women, this paper examines both the nature of the problems faced by Eastern European countries and the USSR in terms of their gender dimension, and of the role and task of national machinery for the advancement of women during the period of transformation and beyond.

Women's issues and restructuring

Analysis of the position of women in the Eastern European countries and the USSR during the current reforms reveals several common tendencies.

First, the number and share of women in decision-making positions has decreased. In Bulgaria the percentage of women in Parliament fell from 21 to 8.5 (elections of June 1990); in Czechoslovakia it feel from 29.5 to 6 (elections of June 1990; in the Germany Democratic Republic, from 32.2 to 20.5 (elections of March 1990); in Hungary, from 20.9 to 7 (elections of March 1990); in Romania, from 34.3 to 3.5.

Secondly, experts have pointed to the existence or threat of unemployment for women in the majority of countries. For example, in 1989, 54.2 per cent of all unemployed persons in Yugoslavia were women. That had been exacerbated by the rise in the number of bankruptcies whereby the legal protection of the employment of mothers of small children and pregnant women could not be guaranteed. A system of unemployment benefits was being elaborated in most of the countries. However, as pointed out by Lumpily Navarova (Czechoslovakia), such a system was only one aspect of State support. More important was the identification of alternative employment and the organized retraining of the unemployed.

Thirdly, women have been largely excluded from national schemes of training and retraining.

Fourthly, strong evidence exists that traditional stereotypes of gender relations have resurfaced. These have been used by high-ranking decision makers in attempts to justify such policies as "women go home".

The mass media is also using materials and images glorifying the "natural predestination of women ". As stated by Slovenka Drakulic (Yugoslavia): "Women's problems are not the issue, except in a case of political manipulation."

Fifthly, images of women's bodies are being exploited. Pornographic and semi-pornographic commercials are considered indicative of political liberalization. Evidence from Czechoslovakia, Hungary, USSR and Yugoslavia suggest that an explosion has occurred in the production of such literature. Sex-shops in the cities, magazines displayed in kiosks, sex on television and phone-call sex have increased.

Sixthly, sexual harassment against women in public and private spheres, sexual abuse of wives and children, and prostitution, previously reported to the Committee on the Elimination of Discrimination against Women as not existing, are a reality. Hungary refers to the rising number of recorded crimes connected with prostitution as indicative of the widening social basis of prostitution.

Lastly, indications exist that women's reproductive rights are threatened. Poland, strongly influenced by the policies of the Catholic church, is an extreme example. A draft law approved by the Senate in September 1990, if approved by the Sejm, would ban abortion. Polish women face immediate and devastating personal losses in addition to losing seats in Parliament. In Hungary, the question has been raised during the election campaign. The Society for Embryo Protection and the Society of Physicians against Abortion has applied to the Constitu-

*   by Anastasia Posadskaya, Head, Gender Studies Centre, Institute for Socio-Economic Studies on Population, USSR Academy of Sciences.

tional Court to place legal restrictions on the prevailing liberal practice. In Yugoslavia, one of the first issues on the political agenda was the restriction of abortion. There was also pressure from the church to ban abortion. East German women petitioned and demonstrated to maintain the existing abortion law. It was only in Romania, where abortion had been virtually banned by the previous regime, that abortion has been legalized.

It is important to note these common features in order to appreciate the complexity of the role and task of national machinery.

Women's issues before restructuring

A similar approach to the solution of the "woman question", based on Marxist concepts, could be identified in each of the countries concerned before restructuring. That approach could be summarized as follows: legal and factual equality in the social position of women and men; widespread and complete participation in public production; transformation of gender relations in the family; and appropriate, purposeful, active politics aimed at achieving those goals.

Legal equality may be a constitutional principle but national machinery for the advancement of women is needed to transform that principle into reality, particularly because traditional (patriarchal) gender relations still exist in the countries of Eastern Europe. In spite of a high level of women's involvement in production, women continued to occupy the lower paid, less prestigious, less creative jobs with low possibilities for vertical professional mobility.

The percentage of women heads of enterprises and organizations has always been negligible but decreased from 6.9 in 1985 to 5.6 in 1989. In 1984, in Czechoslovakia the average female wage was 68.9 per cent of the male wage and in 1988, 70.9 per cent. Similarly, the average salary for women in Yugoslavia was lower than for men in all branches of economic activity. Romanian women accounted for 80 per cent of all people earning the minimum wage and less then 2 per cent of the higher wage group. Gender relations in the family and the sexual division of housework remained unchanged. In the USSR, women worked (production and home work) on average 76.3 hours per week compared to 59.4 hours for men. The phenomenon of women's double load arose, discrediting notions of both women's emancipation and gender equality and producing the myth of women's "over-emancipation"

It may be concluded that traditional relations in society have been strengthened, relegating women to "her" duties within the family, which were thus reproduced at a societal level. That should be borne in mind when examining the role and task of both the old and the new national machinery for the advancement of women.

The national machinery of Eastern European countries and the Union of Soviet Socialist Republics before restructuring

The Seminar on National Machinery for Monitoring and Improving the Status of Women was held at Vienna, from 28 September to 2 October 1987. The Seminar defined a national machinery as "a single body or a complex organized system of bodies, often under different authorities, but recognized by the Government as the institution dealing with the promotion of the status of women".

Prior to the period of reform, national machinery in each country had many similar features. Each held the status of a non-governmental organization and most, although holding the right to propose legislation, had only formal autonomous status and were in practice dependent on the policy of the ruling party. Most of these organizations were established during the Second World War as part of the Antifascist Front, but they gradually evolved into bureaucratic women's organizations not engaged in finding solutions to women's issues because those issues were proclaimed to have been solved. Independent women's organizations did not exist. Thus national machinery was neither strong enough nor prepared to raise issues for public debate, either generally or within the context of the implementation of the Convention on the Elimination of All Forms of Discrimination against Women. Reports to the Committee were not regarded as learning tools or as a means of disseminating information on the implementation of the Convention.

Most countries have already submitted two reports to the Committee on the Elimination of Discrimination against Women on the implementation of the Convention. As noted by the experts on the Committee, the second periodic reports were often merely a repetition of the initial report. These reports were not based on the statistical information necessary for good analysis. Neither were the basic notions - discrimination and equality - of the Convention discussed. Emphasis has always been placed on achievements at the expense of unsolved problems.

Finally, the majority of articles of the Convention (articles 5, 6, 7, 8, 15, 16) were largely ignored. In contrast article 4 of the Convention (temporary special measures aimed at accelerating de facto equality between men and women) was often used to justify the so-called privileges of women in production due to their "natural" roles as mother and housewife. For example, Hungary reported in 1986 that a new set of State provisions to support families with children had been introduced "in order to stimulate fertility and to make women stay at home for the sake of children's caring and rearing". That illustrated a misunderstanding and wrong usage of article 4 and brought about violation of article 5, which required States parties to the Convention to modify the social and cultural patterns of conduct of men and women.

It may be concluded that the national machinery of the countries of Eastern Europe and the USSR are largely invisible and ignore, either explicitly or implicitly, issues of equality of women and men and do not base their work on reliable and comprehensive statistical information. The national machinery could itself be viewed as part of the problem.

Changes in the national machinery of the Eastern European countries and the Union of Soviet Socialist Republics undergoing restructuring

The period of reform in Eastern European countries has opened to them possibilities of adaptation, based on a realistic analysis of the situation of women, and on the experiences of Western countries. Those experiences show that it is useful to establish a separate and autonomous governmental agency to formulate policy regarding women's affairs: a national machinery for the advancement of women. Prior to the process of the restructuring of Eastern European countries, the Commission on the Status of Women had drafted a resolution that underlined the importance of national machinery and requested Governments to provide adequate political, financial and human resources to ensure its effective functioning. Signatories to the Convention were recommended to set up such machinery. The question was what kind of national machinery was adequate to meet the challenges posed by the current period of transition and what should be its priorities.

The fate of the various official women's organizations after the reforms was also similar to that of the national machinery: they either ceased to exist, like the Czechoslovak Council of Women and the National Council of Women in Romania, or they maintained their formal existence and adapted to the new situation. In addition, numerous new independent women's organizations appeared, but they were usually small, and lacked financial resources and other forms of institutional assistance.

A comparison of the structure of the old national machinery with the current ones shows that, in countries such as the German Democratic Republic and the USSR, they have undergone substantial changes. In other countries the old bodies were closed. It was only in the USSR that a new governmental body appeared: a department on the position of women, protection of family, maternity and childhood located within the Cabinet of Ministers. National machinery was also established in the Council of Ministers of the USSR and in the legislative and executive bodies of the republics. Again, none of the relevant bodies explicitly dealt with issues of gender equality and equal opportunities for women and men in all spheres of public and private life.

In countries where national machinery is undergoing transformation and in countries where it has not changed or is disappearing, the situation of women has deteriorated. That is indicative of the importance not only of the bodies themselves but also of the provision of resources commensurate with their tasks.

It seems reasonable in the period of restructuring that national machinery should also be restructured. The difficulty lies in identifying appropriate directions, forms and strategies to assist in that process. Bearing in mind the potential of national machinery to ensure that issues of equality are considered when formulating policy, it is crucial that the decision-making process at both the political and administrative levels is clearly enunciated. The following steps are considered essential:

(a) Ideological reappraisal of State policy towards women;

(b) Setting-up an effective information system for monitoring developments in women's issues, countrywide;

(c) Deciding on the level of operation of national machinery, within the governmental structure;

(d) Establishing links with and provision of support to the new women's organizations;

(e) Building a positive environment;

(f) Supporting a broad range of research programmes on women including establishing gender and women's studies courses within the education system.

Ideological reappraisal of State policy on women

During the period of socio-economic and political restructuring every country needs to reappraise State policy on women. That may take a number of forms including an official statement or the formulation of a position paper. New approaches to such State policy are currently being formulated in Czechoslovakia, Hungary and the USSR.

The theoretical basis for the elaboration of a policy on women and the definition of major priorities are of particular importance in the formulation of a position paper that contains a critical overview of the previous policy on women. The position paper should also include a discussion of gender equality and discrimination in order to put them back on the political agenda. The social as opposed to the biological determination of gender relations might be pointed out. Furthermore, the principle of the sovereignty of all the elements of the social structure - personality, gender, family, production unit, community, region, nation - should be stressed. Transition from policy based on the ideology of protectionism to policy based on the ideology of personal autonomy

might be suggested and elaborated. The document might be organized according to urgent medium- and long-term goals and should emphasize the notion of gender equality.

The position paper might propose the establishment of a special governmental body to be used by women in the restructuring processes. Hopefully the title and the functions of this body would help to overcome the traditional linkage of women with issues of family and childhood. That body might be called the Council on the Equal Status of Women and Men. Finally, an important issue is the quota system. In the past that system has enabled a high percentage of women to be represented at the various levels of decision-making. When the quota system was lifted the share of women in all the power structures fell dramatically. Quotas could be re-established based on new principles: the reintroduction of quotas to be decided by the relevant organization, not a superior one; men should also be covered by this provision in areas where they are underrepresented.

Information system for monitoring developments in women's status

The function of national machinery for the advancement of women would be only symbolic if it did not create the information system necessary for monitoring developments in women's status.

The first problem is to overcome the resistance of information producers to the production of gender-disaggregated data. The second problem relates to the first in that the compilation of statistics on the situation of women is only in its infancy worldwide. Although the first steps in that direction have been taken, most notably by United Nations bodies, the most decisive work should be performed at the national level, in particular in the Eastern European countries and the USSR. The provision of regular and reliable information on women is necessary for

monitoring developments in women's status. A major effort is required to ensure that such information is published regularly and taken into account when formulating policy so that women's perspective is integrated in the development strategy.

In conclusion, there is no ideal or easy prescription to solve the "woman question" or to set up national machinery to effectively deal with the question. It depends solely on the people who are building the national machinery as to whether it will remain an ineffective bureaucratic mechanism or become a flexible and developing structure responsive to the needs of the people. Above all, the construction of national machinery should be creative.

III. A COMPARATIVE ANALYSIS OF WOMEN'S INDUSTRIAL PARTICIPATION DURING THE TRANSITION FROM CENTRALLY PLANNED TO MARKET ECONOMIES IN EAST CENTRAL EUROPE*

Historical background: prior to the transition period

Economic, social and political context

Within the economies of state socialist countries, broadly defined as centrally planned or command economies, certain distinguishing features can be identified. Of central importance for women's industrial participation is the concentration on heavy industry, to the detriment of consumer-led production and of the service sector.

All of the state socialist countries of east central Europe are nominally in favour of women's emancipation with very early legislation on equal pay for women. That commitment is expressed in social welfare measures to facilitate women's labour-force participation. Most of those measures concern child-care facilities and some attempts to socialize domestic labour, though the level of provision differs widely between countries.

Some analysts claim that the Governments of east central European countries instituted those measures simply to increase women's labour force participation. Many researchers feel that they were driven by economic imperatives in the situation of scarce labour after the Second World War, and not primarily by a commitment to equality for women. Yet such legislation and social welfare measures have offered women some degree of choice. Generous maternity leave and child-care benefits have made it possible for women to decide whether and when to have children, and when to return to the work-force.

Maternity-leave provisions varied between countries during the post-War period, and manifested contradictory trends in the Polish case that could be read as economistic responses to fluctuations in the demand for labour. The most generous of those provisions were the so-called "baby year" in the German Democratic Republic and the three years' partially paid leave in Hungary, with 18 weeks paid and up to three years unpaid leave in Poland. Women's jobs had to be kept open for them during their absence on maternity leave. Not many women in Hungary took advantage of the full three-year period,

however, since the level of pay was not sufficient to substitute for labour-force participation. Many women returned to work early, or worked in the second economy to supplement the child-care allowance.

Child-care facilities for pre-school-age children were criticized, after the events of autumn 1989, for their unfavourable pupil-teacher ratio, degree of regimentation and lack of individual attention. The level of availability of child-care places differed widely, being very low in Poland (compared to Western European countries) and extremely high in the German Democratic Republic.

In all those countries the level of female labour force participation was very high in comparison with Western Europe, with women accounting for almost 50 per cent of the total labour force. The problem for women lay, however, in the fact that they were legislatively defined as workers and mothers. There was no equivalent definition of men as workers and fathers. That definition structurally enshrined a dual role for women. Indeed, many analysts speak of a triple role resulting from considerable pressure on women to play a part in social or political organizations, on top of paid labour and unpaid domestic work.[1]

Throughout east central Europe, women remained responsible for the overwhelming majority of child-care and household work. In Hungary and the Germany Democratic Republic, for example, surveys showed that women were responsible for 75 per cent of domestic labour. That meant that fully employed women spent an additional 2-3 hours per day on household chores in the German Democratic Republic. In Czechoslovakia women were away from their homes with work, travel to work, and shopping for 9.5-10 hours every working day, and that was before they began to cook or look after children. Some more equitable sharing of domestic duties may have begun in the German Democratic Republic. Nevertheless, *Frauenreport 90* [2] stressed that women were still responsible for the majority of household work.

---

* by Barbara Einhorn, School of European Studies, University of Sussex, Brighton, United Kingdom of Great Britain and Northern Ireland, and Swasti Mitter, Brighton Business School, Brighton Polytechnic, United Kingdom.

[1] B. Einhorn, "Socialist Emancipation: the Women's Movement in the GDR", in: S. Kruks, R. Rapp, M. Young (eds). *Promissory Notes: Women in the Transition to Socialism* (New York, Monthly Review Press), 1989.

[2] G. Winkler (ed), *Frauenreport 90*, (Berlin, Verlag Die Wirtschaft), 1990.

The double or triple burden meant that women in east-central Europe suffered severe stress and overwork. That over-burdening was exacerbated by the necessity of standing in queues to procure the ingredients for the family meal, not to speak of getting shoes mended and other scarce services. As a result women often perceived - particularly seen in retrospect - the right to work as an obligation, a duty in addition to their family responsibilities, rather than a right they could positively enjoy. In addition, many social welfare benefits were conditional upon labour-force participation, thus increasing the obligatory aspect of going to work.

Very few women had the opportunity to work part-time to alleviate that stress level. That stemmed in part from the heavy demand for labour in most of those economies, in part from their own feeling that a full-time wage was necessary to maintain the household budget. That was especially true for female-headed households, of which there was a very high proportion due to the high divorce rates. As a result, in 1986 only 6 per cent of female workers in Poland and 7.6 per cent in Czechoslovakia worked part-time. By 1989, the percentage for Czechoslovakia had risen to 11.6 per cent. However, 23-27 per cent of all women workers and 40 per cent of women returning to work after maternity leave stated they would prefer to work part-time.

Female labour-force participation in Western Europe had also risen since 1970. Yet it remained considerably lower on average than in east-central Europe, with women accounting for around 35-40 per cent of the work-force in the West compared with 40-50 per cent in the East. It was worth noting, however, that a far higher percentage of the female labour force in Western Europe worked part-time, in 1985 for example, 44 per cent in the United Kingdom, 53 per cent in the Netherlands and 30 per cent in the Federal Republic of Germany.

Women bringing up children on their own in east-central Europe struggled to make ends meet, despite some positive discrimination in terms of child-care benefits, access to child-care facilities and annual leave. As a result of stress levels and child-care constraints all women, but especially single mothers, tended to choose less demanding jobs, involving less skilled work than their level of qualification, and hence relatively low pay.

The high proportion of female-headed households created a large cohort of lone female pensioners. Women also tended to live a remarkable average of 7 years longer than men in most of the countries under discussion, which increased the size of that cohort. Old-age pensions were generally low, providing on average only about 50 per cent of earned income. Many women received only the basic pension due to their relatively lower paid employment.

Many therefore felt obliged to continue working past retirement age. The transition period was likely to have specific implications for that group of women.

There were benefits and costs in female labour-force participation under State socialism. Going out to work was taken for granted for the 40-odd years of the socialist experiment in Eastern Europe. The restructuring process needed to shed labour and tended to eliminate the notion of labour-force participation as the norm for women. The return to the family as women's primary sphere of responsibility would have profound repercussions for women. Not only would it undermine their economic independence, it would also affect their confidence and self-image, and their perception of their social role. That in turn would influence gender relations within the family and have attitudinal and behavioural implications for the education of the future generation.

Pre-transition employment patterns for women

The general emphasis on heavy industry meant that there were structural reasons for women's disadvantaged position in the industrial labour market. Socialist realist ideologists promoted stereotyped images of a woman driving a tractor, or wearing a hard hat on a building site. Yet most women employed in heavy industry tended to be in the over-staffed clerical and low-grade administrative branches within that industry.

Occupational segregation in turn had immediate implications in terms of salary, since it was skilled industrial workers in heavy industry who comprised the elite of those economies in term of earning power. As a result of their location in administrative and similar jobs women earned less than their male colleagues. For example, even women working as production workers within industry earned on average 12 per cent less take-home pay than their male counterparts.

Women workers were heavily concentrated in those jobs requiring lower levels of qualification and responsibility. Although the level of women's qualifications increased over time in several countries, far fewer women than men performed skilled work in industry.

Despite the early legislation on equal pay, statistics made more widely available after the end of the old régimes showed substantial discrepancies in wages, in all sectors of the economy. Paradoxically, the gap between men's and women's wages turned out to be not so different from Western wage differentials. In most countries women earned on average between 66 and 75 per cent of men's wages.

In the economies of all State socialist countries, there was a high level of occupational segregation.

Women tended to be concentrated in some sectors of the economy such as light industry, textiles, the retail trade or the service sector, all of which paid lower wages than did the prioritized heavy industry or construction sectors. Women were underrepresented in both of those areas.

In addition, young women tended to choose traditionally female occupations. That trend contradicted both officially proclaimed equality of educational opportunity and the widely held notion that education would overcome discrimination on the basis of gender.

In all the countries under consideration, girls' educational qualifications at school-leaving exceeded those of boys. In Czechoslovakia, Hungary and Poland, however, no single unified school system for boys and girls existed. In those countries, girls tended to graduate from a humanities-oriented general secondary school, while more boys had already completed training in a vocational secondary school. Hence girls in those countries entered the labour market at a disadvantage. They were thus structurally more likely to work in unskilled jobs within industry from the very beginning of their working lives, and not merely later as a result of a broken career structure due to maternity leave or other factors.

Women formed a high percentage or even the majority of the work-force in several formerly male-dominated professions including engineering, medicine and law. As those professions became feminized, there was a tendency for them to become devalued in terms of status and remuneration. It also resulted in the use of quotas for female entry to professions such as medicine ostensibly to counteract excessive feminization, yet such quotas were never applied to other over-feminized professions such as nursing or child-care.[3/]

The proportion of women diminished towards the upper levels of the career hierarchy within feminized professions, similar to Western Europe. Only 14 per cent of the total female labour force in Czechoslovakia in 1989 held management positions. Of those, 65 per cent were in lower-level management, 25 per cent in mid-level management, and only 10 per cent in top management.[4/] The number of women holding top management positions in Poland

was 4.5 per cent in 1988.[5/] The German Democratic Republic typically had relatively high levels of women managers in light industry, postal and telecommunications, and the retail trade.

Structural as well as socio-cultural reasons contributed to a situation where women themselves were less likely to take on management positions, and men saw them as unsuitable candidates. According to working-class women interviewed in the German Democratic Republic, in 1988, they took paid sick-leave to look after children in 78 per cent of cases, even though legislation provided for either parent to do so.[6/] Women's absence from work to care for sick children, and on extended maternity leave, contributed to the view of women as "unreliable" workers.

Women had less leisure time at their disposal than men due to their primary or exclusive responsibility for domestic labour. That hindered their capacity for further study to improve their qualifications, with negative consequences for their career prospects. In the Hungarian case, the expansion of the second economy during the 1980s meant increasingly that men did two or three paid jobs while women were thrown back even more heavily onto domestic responsibilities, often including the additional work of tending the family private plot for cash sale. That again limited career development.

The underrepresentation of women at the top of career hierarchies was mirrored in political representation. There were great discrepancies between their level of trade union or party membership and their representation in higher decision-making bodies. Although women were well represented in parliament, important decisions were taken in the upper echelons of the ruling party not in parliament. Significantly, women were almost entirely absent from the Politburos of the parties. One of the many paradoxes of the transitional period was that the level of female representation in all the new democratically elected parliaments of Eastern Europe dropped dramatically. That had negative implications for the promotion of women's rights and retraining needs during the process of democratization and economic restructuring. It is important to monitor whether the newly emerging women's movements will improve the level of women's representation in the near future.

[3/]   J. Heinen, The Impact of Social Policy on the Behaviour of Women Workers in Poland and East Germany, In: *Critical Social Policy*, Issue 29, vol. 10, No. 2, 1990.

[4/]   A. Kroupova, Women, Employment and Earnings in Central and East European Countries, Paper to Tripartite Symposium on Equality of Opportunity and Treatment for Men and Women in Employment in Industrialized Countries, Prague, May, 1990.

[5/]   Gontarczyk-Wesola, Country Report Poland, 1989.

[6/]   *Frauenreport 90*, ibid.

The transition period

<u>Major problems affecting or constraining industrial development in the transition economy</u>

The transition period presents opportunities, but also high costs. All of the countries concerned are experiencing high inflation and rising prices, decline in real wages and the loss of subsidies on rent, basic foods, transport, child-care and children's clothes.

Industrial restructuring is bringing about the closure of entire industries that cannot compete on the world market. The textile industry in Czechoslovakia, eastern Germany and Poland is one example. The brown-coal industry in Czechoslovakia, eastern Germany and Poland is an industry that is collapsing because of the massive environmental damage it has caused as well as its lack of economic viability. Technical obsolescence is crippling the automobile industry in Czechoslovakia and in eastern Germany in comparison with its environmentally conscious western German and Japanese competitors using robot assembly methods. Similarly, micro-technology in the German Democratic Republic, which had "re-invented" the microchip in order to save on scarce hard currency, cannot now compete with Western equivalents.

The agricultural production cooperatives (LPGs) in eastern Germany, formerly show-pieces of socialist-style agriculture that offered their members a high standard of living and total social security, are now unable to compete against more attractive western German and Dutch dairy products, meat and vegetables, and especially hitherto unavailable imported exotic fruits. In September 1990, vegetables were being ploughed back into the soil in the German Democratic Republic. Changes in ownership patterns and in legislation contributed to delays in much-needed foreign investment. Local capital was virtually non-existent. A voucher system for creating credit to enable workers or others to become enterprise owners would contribute to inflationary pressure, thereby undermining stabilization of those economies.

Removing subsidies on basic foods, rents and services was clearly necessary. However, in the short-term, faced with rising prices it will compound the problems of unemployment. There is a shortage of professional skills needed to implement market methods. Expert advice is required so that assets, land and property are not undersold in the process of privatization. Daimler-Benz, for example, purchased the Potsdamer Platz site in Berlin - a prime site in the probable future capital - at an extremely low price. Firms hard-pressed to retrench are tending to ignore the relevant labour laws (where those laws have not already been abolished) that guarantee women's jobs during maternity leave and prohibit enterprises from sacking pregnant women.

<u>Recent trends in women's employment and unemployment</u>

It is imperative to gather much more detailed empirical data than is presently available to facilitate a breakdown of the unemployment figures by sex, industrial sector and skill level. This is necessary in order to understand the implications of current patterns of female unemployment in relation to future employment opportunities. The restructuring process is still in its early stages, especially in Czechoslovakia, which explains the relatively low rate of unemployment there at present. Trends are beginning to emerge, but it will be some time before clear patterns become evident. Joint East-West research, with Western partners providing conceptual and methodological approaches that can be tested on empirical data from east-central Europe, would be ideal. Monitoring the impact of the current transition period on patterns of female labour-force participation is essential.

Unemployment, as opposed to underemployment, was virtually unknown in east-central Europe prior to 1989. An exception was Hungary, where 16,000 people registered unemployed in the first quarter of 1988, 40 per cent of them women. Unemployment is rising sharply in all countries, with a tendency for women to form the majority of the unemployed. Women accounted for 46 per cent of those unemployed in Slovenia in 1990; for 51 per cent of the unemployed in Poland in October 1990; for 54 per cent of people unemployed in the German Democratic Republic in January 1991, and for 69.4 per cent of those unemployed in Bulgaria in November 1990. Czechoslovakia had a low level of 1.9 per cent unemployment in February 1991, scarcely having begun the predicted sharp restructuring process. The prognosis for 1992 is 36,000-80,000 unemployed women, and that women are likely to comprise 66 per cent of those unemployed in the future.

Some of the industries and sectors of the economy worst hit by closures, such as textiles and light industry, are those employing a high concentration of women.

There are marked regional and gender imbalances in unemployment levels. East Berlin has an unemployment rate of 10.9 per cent, while an almost 100 per cent female unemployment rate exists around industrial towns such as Zwickau and Cottbus, former centres for textiles and light industry.[7] Huge regional dislocation would occur if the threatened closure of Rostock's shipyards occurs. Unemployment levels throughout the Germany Democratic Republic are said to have reached 50 per cent by June 1991.

Those men who are fit and skilled are already beginning a mass long-term commute - a new form of guest-worker who returns home to eastern Germany at the weekend. Already 20,000 east Germans a month are seeking work in the western part of the country. This trend means that there could be major demographic distortions, with the elderly, the young and the women who care for both these groups left behind in an industrial wasteland in eastern Germany.

In Poland there are severe regional imbalances. In Czechoslovakia, the region of northern Bohemia has been described by some observers as a moon landscape as a result of open-cast brown coal mining. In that region as well as in the southeast of eastern Germany and in Silesia in Poland, the closure of brown-coal mines and the heavily polluting, inefficient processing industries dependent on them would produce very high levels of unemployment.[8]

Female unemployment in heavy industry and mining, and closures in the textile industry, together with a lack of alternative sources in light industry for female employment, has led to severe gender imbalances in the level of unemployment. At the end of October 1990 there were 37.3 unemployed women for one workplace compared with 9.5 men. In six regional districts, there were 100 women for every job opening. In one district that figure reached 1,398 women for one job. That was equivalent to there being no job offer available for 97.3 per cent of registered unemployed women. Young women are especially badly affected throughout Poland. In the German Democratic Republic, young women are suffering particularly acute unemployment levels. Female school-leavers are experiencing considerable difficulties in finding apprenticeships or places at universities and colleges.

It seems that many east-central European women are accepting redundancy on a short-term basis, often looking forward to the opportunity of spending more time with their children. However, they have no experience that could allow them to sense the danger that taking a few years off could turn into long-term unemployment. Neither do they have experience of the material and psychological effects of unemployment.

The impact of the transition on women's industrial participation

In the future, it is possible that new technology and expansion of the service sector may create new employment opportunities for women. In the short-term, however, women are particularly badly affected by economic restructuring, with high levels of unemployment.

There are numerous retraining schemes available. In the German Democratic Republic, those are insufficient to meet the demand. In west Berlin, private sector retraining and institutes for further education charge high fees and give course certificates that are not recognized by possible employers. Computer courses seem to be the only ones specifically aimed at women, restricting them to secretarial positions enhanced by new technology. Much retraining is narrowly focused in terms of economic restructuring. Courses offered include word-processing, marketing, distribution, taxation, banking and accountancy. Many women tend to choose non-vocational courses, such as counselling, how to orient themselves in the new and unfamiliar job market or how to present themselves for interview.

One potentially serious problem is that many job advertisements, and even some retraining courses, specify people aged between 30 and 47. Older women who do not qualify for early retirement (age 57) are thus disadvantaged. Job centres require applicants to be readily available at any time for interviews or to start work. When women become unemployed, the crèche/nursery school withdraws their child-care place, hence it becomes difficult for them to be readily available.

Child-care facilities are themselves under threat. Enterprises seeking to make themselves competitive tend to shed the enterprise crèche or nursery school with ease, sloughing them off onto near bankrupt local authorities. Alternatively, steeply increased fees mean that many women can no longer afford child-care. Other social security support measures are also threatened. The system of polyclinics in the German Democratic Republic, which ensured that women automatically had regular check-ups, pregnancy checks and so on, is being dissolved in favour of private medical practices. That may well mean a deterioration in service for some women, especially rural women. Reproductive rights, in particular abortion rights, are also being threatened in most of the countries of east central Europe.

---

[7] M. Beyer, Interview with B. Einhorn, March 11, 1991.

[8] Moserova, Interview with B. Einhorn, Prague, September, 1990.

One of the positive approaches to enhancing women's employment and career opportunities is in training courses for management. There is a general reluctance evident in women's attitudes towards management responsibilities, overburdened as they are with their triple role. Results of a recent Soviet survey conducted for the International Labour Organisation (ILO) in the city of Naberejnye Chelny indicates, however, that such reluctance may be viewed as a general legacy of the command economy with its undervaluation of individual responsibility. Only 8 per cent of men and 3 per cent of women in the sample aspired to become managers. That low motivation was echoed by the substantial number - 40 per cent of men and 50 per cent of women - who prefer to remain rank and file workers, albeit with some creative content to their work. Sixty-eight per cent of men and 72 per cent of women stated positively that they had no intention of becoming managers.2/ In Hungary, too, women seem reluctant to become entrepreneurs. In 1988, 36 per cent of men (41 per cent of single men) but only 16 per cent of women expressed the wish to become entrepreneurs.10/

Entrepreneurship opportunities, as promoted by Dr. Tatiana Lukianenko's Women's Association Mission in Moscow, could offer valuable experience in establishing training courses for women wanting to set up in business. The solution of self-employment seems much favoured by policy makers right across Europe, and has the advantage of developing resourcefulness and individual initiative, neither of which were rewarded under State socialism. However, as a policy for retraining and redeployment in the process of economic restructuring it should not be overestimated or relied upon too exclusively.

There is a special need for training courses that would enable women to move into industries using new technology. A Hungarian study suggests that the new technologies tend to exacerbate the gender-specific division of labour. On the basis of that study, it could be speculated that where new technology requires skill rather than manual dexterity, men would tend to move into formerly female-dominated occupations and that, conversely, as robotization deskills some formerly male-dominated occupations, men would desert them and be replaced by women.

An enormous cycle of social dislocation is emerging, with particular implications for women. A rise in alcoholism and consequent violence within marriage, a sharp increase in the rate of suicide, and usage of marriage counselling centres and newly established women refuges are a few examples. Unemployment is also changing the institution of marriage itself. It is once again becoming an economic unit, that women feel insecure about leaving. Labour-force participation and relative economic independence had meant that marriage had lost that function but the new situation has increased women's dependency.

It will be important, in this situation, to ensure that women benefit from increased employment opportunities. Research and training should thus relate to the specific needs of women workers. In a plan for the advancement of women, it is important to stress the significance of women's increased role not only in the unskilled and semi-skilled professions but also in the higher levels of technical and managerial jobs. It is important for initiating women-specific bias in development; for providing role models for young women; and for utilizing effectively the cognitive skills that those countries so desperately need.

Emerging skill requirements and opportunities for women in management

Changes in the legal structures of business enterprises: need for skills in finance and accountancy

Future employment opportunities for women (and men) in the industrial sector will depend on a country's ability to emerge from the transitional phase with a viable manufacturing base. One of the major obstacles to achieving that goal lies in the inexperience of the East European countries with the types of managerial and financial expertise that are required in a market economy. An orientation to those skills is particularly important as the legal and organiza-

tional structure of business enterprises change in the move towards privatization and decentralization. In centrally planned economies, companies were owned by everybody and were controlled on behalf of the people by a bureaucratic State apparatus, responsible only to the party. Companies were not allowed to go bankrupt even if they were grossly inefficient. Investments were made without much regard to returns. In contrast, the dominant structure of firms in the market economy is the joint-stock company, in which ownership is based on the holding of shares by private savers. The shares can be bought and sold but, if

---

2/ A. Posadskaya and N. Zakharova, "To be a manager: changes for women in the USSR", report for the International Labour Organisation, 1990.

10/ G. Lengyel, Entrepreneurial Inclinations. In: *Research Review* on Hungarian Social Sciences, No. 3, 1989.

retained, hold the possibility of an annual dividend. Companies in a market economy are autonomous but strictly controlled by the discipline of the capital market. Creditors can start bankruptcy proceedings to close a non-profitable company.

There are many other forms of business enterprise in a market economy. Some companies are owned wholly or in part by their workforce. Some, generally small, companies are privately held and their shares are not traded on the stock market. Some State-owned companies are, in contrast, publicly quoted on stock exchanges and a proportion of their shares are held privately. Hence, the essential characteristic of a market economy is not private ownership but the existence of a capital market where investors are able to determine where to put their savings. The core of the capital market is the stock exchange where company shares are traded. It obliges companies to compete for investment resources through the maximization of profits and of the value of their assets. The existence of a competitive market for joint-stock companies establishes a point of reference for all other companies, including those that are State-owned or have workers as directors on the Board of Management.[11]/

The different business tradition of Eastern Europe renders a smooth transition to a market economy difficult. The efficient working of the stock exchange and capital market requires an understanding of a complex array of financial institutions and policies. The countries lack much-needed experience and expertise, particularly in the areas of accountancy, finance and insurance. If expertise in management and finance is to play a crucial role in achieving efficiency in the post-transitional phase, a case could be made for targeting women for delivering the necessary skills. In Eastern European countries, women have long had a visible presence in the field of accountancy. In Poland, for example, over 80 per cent of accountants are women. In a centrally planned economy, however, the profession involved very little skill beyond bookkeeping and hence did not have the high status usually given to it within the Economic Community. With Eastern Europe's move towards a market economy, however, the status of the profession is poised for a change. At that juncture, if given access to relevant training, women, as existing practitioners, stand a good chance of augmenting their position in that growing and crucial area of expertise.

Women's future in personnel management

In the post-transitional phase, the field of personnel management would assume a key position in business units. A transition to a market economy demands recruitment and pay on the basis of a worker's productivity. Hence, the assessment, development and utilization of human resources will form a strategic part of an overall management exercise. In the West, women have made successful careers in that field of management, often at a very senior level. It is accepted that women's skill in dealing with people is an asset in situations where the companies attempt to recruit and retain the most relevant skills. It is possible that such a positive image of women could be cultivated to promote women's opportunities in the field of personnel and human-resource planning in the East European countries.

Integration in the global market: need for marketing skills

One of the main features of East Europe's transitional phase has been the economic de-linking of the Council for Mutual Economic Assistance (CMEA) from the Soviet economy. The agreements granting Czechoslovakia, Hungary and Poland association links with the European Communities (EC) were expected to be signed in the autumn of 1991. Bulgaria and Romania, likewise, have been negotiating trade and cooperation agreements with EC. A new market in EC offers prospects and problems for the East European countries. Relatively unfettered access to an affluent market could be highly conducive to growth, but hurdles have to be overcome in order to benefit from those new opportunities. The current recession in the West renders the market in Europe highly competitive, not only in terms of price but also in terms of variety and quality.

For a company's success, managing the market is becoming just as important as its availability. Skill in advertising is an asset in the changed climate; so is skill in the management of fashion and design. In Eastern Europe, women have a long tradition of involvement in handicraft and designs. In the post-transitional phase of the market economy, those traditional skills could be harnessed to cater to the differentiated and discriminating markets of the EC. The same expertise in marketing and design could also cater to the rising expectation of consumers in the domestic economies. The use of design as a competitive strategy requires skills in information technology because computer-aided design/computer-aided manufacturing (CAD/CAM) reduced the importance of conceptual skills and increased the role of computing in the field of design. Women's industrial employment opportunities depend as much on their ability to gain access to training in information technology as in the areas of management and marketing. United Nations agencies could play an

---

[11]/ ICFTU, Women Workers in Poland, Appendix 61/W/3(b), 5th World Conference, Ottawa, April, 1991.

active role by facilitating the transference of knowledge and experience from West European countries where women have managed to augment their share in business by combining their designing skills with cost effective use of information technology.[12]/

Organizational innovations and opportunities for women in self employment

The breaking up of State enterprises has led to confusion and chaos in the transitional period. Yet, it is possible to envisage the emergence of some positive outcomes of decentralization in the post-transitional phase of these countries. The organizational structure of industrial districts in central and northeast Italy could provide a model for such innovations. Small-scale enterprises in those industrial districts could act as subcontractors of retailing or manufacturing companies. Whereas the market is assessed and controlled by larger organizations, the small companies supply, quickly and flexibly, the sub-assembled or finished goods on a subcontracting basis. That efficient network between the main company and satellite enterprises, described as flexible specialization, offers opportunities for self-employment among those who do not possess either sizeable capital or marketing expertise. Significantly, regional governments in Italy supply small companies with technical, business and other institutional facilities.[13]/

Despite the bureaucracy of a centrally planned economy, the tradition of small business in East Europe has survived among small-scale rural entrepreneurs and urban street vendors in Hungary and Poland. In the unregulated economy of the Eastern European countries, women have always been visible as competent traders. A sustainable enterprise culture in the post-transitional period could thus be planned on the strength of women's existing entrepreneurial skills. Their ability to move from informal business activities to viable and legal small businesses, however, would depend on their access to financial assistance from regional and national governments; technical assistance from international agencies; training in accounting and financial skills; and training in personnel management.

Foreign direct investment and women's opportunities in small enterprises

Foreign direct investment in the transitional phase of Eastern Europe has been exceedingly small. In theory, the exceptionally low wage rates and relatively skilled work-force of countries such as Hungary and Poland should make them attractive manufacturing bases for multinational companies. Yet

even Hungary and Poland have so far managed to attract only a handful of major projects. In contrast, the success rate has been higher in enticing small-venture capital from foreign companies. The inexperience with capital markets makes big investments appear risky to foreign companies. For small collaborative projects, the liberalization of foreign investment rules has compensated to a certain extent for the lack of a structured capital market in the Eastern European countries.

An enterprise culture based on foreign collaboration has provided an alternative to the export-processing-zone model of industrialization, adopted so vigorously in the past decade in many developing countries. With increased introduction of computer technology in the production process, the role of cheap and semi-skilled female labour in the manufacturing process is in sharp decline. In that climate, it would not be easy for the Eastern European countries to entice foreign investment in export-processing zones merely with a promise of low wages for their employees. In order to cater to the discriminating market of the United States of America and Western Europe, the transnational companies need cognitive skills and flexible training. The large corporations are more ready to engage in direct investment when the recipient countries provide large domestic markets; adequate infrastructure; the requisite skills, increasingly in the fields of high technology; and management expertise, including that in human-resource development.

Those are precisely the facilities and skills that the Eastern European countries do not adequately possess. Hence, in the transitional phase it is the small foreign venture capital in the feminized light industries that could stimulate growth and the transference of technology. In order to exploit the potential of foreign-venture capital, priorities should be accorded to building regional supporting institutions so that foreign investors could find attractive local partners; and small local companies could act as important suppliers of specialized components for their foreign collaborators.

Small businesses could be set up without large initial capital and women could thus achieve a degree of flexibility in working hours. A model for economic regeneration based on self-employment and small businesses offers possibilities for women's advancement in the sphere of paid work. But their actual progress depends critically on evolving a set of industrial policies that encourage and assist women in gaining skills in self-management and personnel management; management of a small business; fi-

---

[12]/ S. Mitter, Computer-aided Manufacturing and Women's Employment, Springer Verlag, 1991, pp. 103-107.

[13]/ Ibid, pp. 188-189.

nance and accountancy; and national and international marketing. United Nations organizations could contribute to a plan for the advancement of women by assisting East European Governments in identifying and funding requisite programmes for women's training.

Environmental clean-up and women's jobs

Recent initiatives in cleaning up the environment have had mixed effects on women's careers. Women have suffered from the loss of employment arising out of closures and the slowing down of industrial activities. The cleaning up initiatives have, however, also brought additional foreign funds into the region, creating new and better employment of women and men. In addition to loans and grants coming from the World Bank and the PHARE programme of EC, there have been initiatives and investment by private specialized Western consultancy companies. Targeted industries for "greening" were generally the ones that traditionally offered employment to women. For example, fish- and vegetable-oil processing in Czechoslovakia is to be adapted to environmentally clean technology. There is also a growing awareness among the same consultancy firms that in order to make greening cost-effective and sustainable, it is important to have the committed involvement of the local people. With a reasonable pool of female and male expertise in the environmentally sound processes of manufacturing, it would be easier for regions to solicit collaboration from foreign companies, who are increasingly keen to project an image of being clean and green.

THE ROADS AHEAD - POLICY ISSUES

Women's responsibility in career planning and networking

The advancement of women in Eastern European countries, as elsewhere, finally depends on women's own initiatives to demand relevant resources for training and skills. Women's participation in the decision-making process likewise hinges on their confidence and commitment to promoting themselves in management positions that are both demanding and time consuming. Their dual role, of mother and worker, has often encouraged women to settle for second best in the world of paid work, in order to improve the quality of their domestic life. The subject of women's role in the world of paid work has evoked contradictory responses from women of this region. The Union of Prague Mothers has defended the desire of women to return to their home. Similarly some women members of the Alliance of Young Democrats in Hungary have viewed the notion of equality as merely adding burdens to women's lives. In a time of economic upheaval, it is especially difficult for a working mother to find the time and energy to prepare herself for management posts while coping with children, shopping and cooking.

There is, however, growing concern that the current economic and political climate is being used to exclude women from decision-making positions. Some activists have warned women of the danger of emphasizing their dual role: the stereotyped image of an over-burdened working mother relegates women to the secondary work-force that is rarely given core jobs with technical and management responsibilities. Unfortunately, in this region women still bear the major burden of domestic work. The appropriate strategy for women's advancement thus lies not in denying the demands of child-care and housework but in stressing the management skills that a working mother has acquired, while balancing her complex roles, particularly in the areas of time management and budgeting. Society's attitudes towards women managers would be easier to change if women themselves could build confidence in their own abilities. The educational programme for women managers thus needs to include not only training in business and new technology but also in confidence building and personal development skills through well-structured leadership and assertiveness training.

Women's networks

It is not easy to formulate management and personal development training programmes for women in a vacuum. The existing East European forums of trade-union leaders and women managers should provide the base for initial networking. The Women's Association Mission in Moscow provides an excellent example. The women members of the newly founded Association of Entrepreneurs in Czechoslovakia, likewise, could initiate similar networking. Leadership and assertiveness training courses for women, as funded by the International Confederation of Trade Unions at Solidarnosc in Poland, could be emulated in other Eastern European countries. Programmes led by trade unions would be particularly important for formulating a demand for positive action for older women who are at the midpoint of their career and who need substantial retraining in order to sustain their positions during restructuring.

Dialogue between the East European countries: the role of government organizations

Each east central European country has its own historical and industrial tradition. There are considerable differences in the experience of the restructuring being felt by the women and men of those countries. Yet there are commonalities as well; hence, there is much to be gained by formulating mechanisms that could facilitate an exchange of experiences of the current adjustment process between those countries. The transfer of knowledge and experience is particularly important for formulating appropriate industrial and human-resource development policies.

Governmental organizations in those countries could play an important role in that direction, not least by complementing the set of actions already taken by the national machinery. The areas where governmental organizations could be particularly effective are in supervising labour market trends and developments, in order to monitor the gaps and redundancies in women's training and skills; initiating training courses that aim to correct the mismatch between the requirements for and availability of women's skills; implementing job-creating methods that would increase women's employment opportunities; extending existing social-support systems (such as child-care facilities, maternity leave) that would enhance women's employment, both in terms of quantity and quality; and in creating institutions for effective wage bargaining.

In the fields of labour policy and work-force planning, there exist some cooperation and networking between Czechoslovakia, Hungary and Poland at a governmental level and those mechanisms could be extended to further the cause of women workers. Cooperation could also be extended to other Eastern European countries. Governmental organizations, by offering relevant institutional support, could be effective in promoting self-employment among women. In most countries, incentives and credit facilities for small-scale entrepreneurs are lacking. It is important that governmental organizations channel their efforts into providing the relevant infrastructure and institutions to ensure that the small business (including self-employment) sector becomes a dynamic one and that the domestic partners are made visible and powerful in foreign joint-ventures. To that end, it would be valuable to have government-sponsored management training courses for women entrepreneurs. It would also be necessary for enterprises to have access to adequate credit facilities. Experiments with new banking facilities are urgently needed.

A simplification of bureaucratic procedures would augment women's opportunities in small-scale entrepreneurship. "One-stop" centres, as promoted in the United States, could provide a model. In those centres, small-scale entrepreneurs are provided with all the relevant information on markets, credit facilities and licensing systems. By simplifying the protocol, the centres have enabled small-scale entrepreneurs to be set up without unnecessary delay and bureaucratic procedures. Cross-national exchanges of experience and learning in that field would be extremely valuable. It is also important to monitor the comparative closure rates of small businesses among women and men entrepreneurs. The monitoring would be useful for identifying special corrective measures that are needed to improve women's chances in the field.

International networking and educational programmes

The networking of women has to transcend regional boundaries. As East Europe establishes linkages with the international market economy, it is vital for Eastern European women to benefit from the professional experiences of women of other countries. Some efforts have been made in Western Europe to facilitate that exchange. Brighton Polytechnic in the United Kingdom, for example, has launched short courses for practising accountants from the East European countries. The courses are not for women only, but the duration of the course and the facilities offered (such as crèche and child care) have been structured with women's needs in mind. Institutional links have already been established with Polish and Czech universities and in time will be extended to other Eastern European countries. Similarly, the current positive action programme in the European Commission for improving the training and business opportunities of women in the field of textiles and clothing could provide a useful model for both the women's networks in Eastern Europe and United Nations agencies. Experts and institutions involved in the EC project could have much to contribute in revitalizing the beleaguered industries of Eastern European countries.

A plan for an integrated action programme

In the light of the above analysis of industrial restructuring, it is possible to formulate an integrated action programme for improving:

(a) The monitoring of women's progress in industrial employment by improved data collection and dissemination;

(b) The formulation of training and educational programmes for providing young women with relevant skills, particularly in new technology;

(c) The implementation of child-care and social-welfare programmes to improve women's job opportunities;

(d) The implementation of retraining programmes for older women to assist them in their career progression and employment opportunities;

(e) The chances of women in management and decision-making posts;

(f) The educational packages that provide women with entrepreneurial skills;

(g) The educational system so that it would encourage young men to share domestic responsibilities;

(h) Networking among women managers and workers within and beyond the national boundaries.

Such an integrated programme would ensure that women benefit not only from the increased opportunities for employment but also from the improved quality of their working lives. The resultant improvement in human resources would benefit countries by strengthening their industrial base and attracting funds from foreign companies. An action programme for the advancement of women could be justified not only on the basis of distributive justice, but also on the grounds of commercial profitability.

Part Two: Country Papers

IV. ALBANIA

A. Albanian women in a new social context*

Albania was the last of the Eastern European countries to embrace the process of economic and political reform. During the early 1960s, Albania severed relations with the Soviet Union and the rest of Eastern Europe. Since that time it has remained outside of every political bloc and for more than two decades was almost entirely isolated, implementing a policy of self-reliance.

This policy has had exceptionally grave consequences for the Albanian economy. From the 1970s onwards Albanian technology became obsolete, Albanian products could not compete on foreign markets and hard-currency funds for capital investments declined. The economy stagnated and living standards dropped to the lowest in Europe. The current situation is the worst of the past three decades. Inflation and unemployment, the existence of which has been acknowledged for the first time, rose and thousands of Albanians sought refuge in foreign embassies in Tirana or, more recently, fled to Greece and Italy. It has become increasingly clear that the only possibility of emerging from this severe economic crisis is by a massive injection of foreign aid and credits. Only then could the economy of Albania be restructured.

In 1985/86, upon the assumption of the Presidency by the new reform leader of the Party of Labour of Albania (PLA), Ramiz Alia, Albanian policy underwent a radical transformation. Alia played a decisive role in the development of political and economic reform in Albania. He was the first to comprehend that the greatest threat to the independence of Albania was poverty and that to avoid this the country must end its isolationist policies and integrate with and develop alongside other European nations. Albanian policy assumed a new, more realistic, orientation.

Economic reform is gradually moving the country towards a market economy, and involves the stimulation of free incentive, privatization of several sectors of the economy and liberalization of prices. Political pluralism has been established, decentralization begun and party functions separated from State functions. Two main problems remain to be solved, but the solution is being debated by the different political forces within the country. Privatization of land in the countryside and the extension of

the private sector in the city could be accomplished either through the total and immediate privatization of the economy or by a gradual transition that allows preparations to be made and the State to maintain a degree of control.

The establishment of political pluralism occurred at a time of economic crisis and coincided with the electoral campaign, which progressed in an atmosphere of social tension. The resultant new political relations and economic and social reform are reflected in the legislation and Constitution of Albania. In September 1990, a Constitutional Commission was created to make the necessary changes and improvements in the Constitution, which is due to be endorsed by the new pluralist Parliament.

Women have played a special role in the process of transformation of Albanian society. The Women's Union of Albania (WUA) was one of the first organizations to become independent from the PLA and to reorient itself as a pluralistic organization, uniting all Albanian women, irrespective of political convictions, in a common cause to gain authentic equality for women with men in all fields of life. WUA also became an independent electoral body in competition for representation in the People's Assembly (the Parliament). The aim of WUA is to directly represent Albanian women in the supreme State organ by actively contributing to improvement and further democratization of legislation, particularly as it relates to the interests of women as wives, mothers and workers. Although, the opposition parties have demanded that only political parties should be allowed to compete in parliamentary elections, the elections on 31 March 1991 saw 74 candidates of WUA competing for seats in the 250-member Parliament.

The past five decades have been a period of awakening and emancipation of Albanian women. Many changes have occurred in the situation of women today compared with 50 years ago. In 1938, the average life expectancy of Albanian women was 38.3 years; only 7 per cent of women were employed; 95 per cent were illiterate and parents had the right to promise their daughter in marriage while she was still a child. Differences of 20, 30 and 40 years of age between spouses were not uncommon. The world of women was the house or village where she lived, and relations with others were strictly controlled and

*   by Fatos Tarifa, Head, Sociological Research Centre, University of Tirana.

limited to members of the immediate family and her own relatives. Society was profoundly patriarchal and women were even prohibited from appearing before men who visited the family. Women were alienated and discriminated against in the family and in society. The situation improved for women through the 1950s, with life expectancy rising to 54.4 years and illiteracy among women under 40 years of age eradicated, and it continued to improve.

Women, who comprise 48.5 per cent of the population, also account for 46.7 per cent of the labour force. The average life expectancy for women is 75.5 years. A genuine revolution has occurred in marriage and family relations. Women play an extremely important role in all spheres of Albanian society, in economic, political and social life. The unwritten laws of the past that relegated women to the lowest position in society have been replaced by democratic legislation that guarantees women equal rights with men in all situations. That legislation conforms with the spirit of international human rights instruments, especially the Convention on the Elimination of All Forms of Discrimination against Women, although Albania has not so far become a signatory to that Convention. The reasons for this are largely bureaucratic and technical, and Albania should soon join the other countries of Eastern Europe and the USSR as a State party to the Convention.

Albanian women enjoy many de jure and de facto rights that women in other countries either have or are fighting for. One of the basics, and the cornerstone of equality, is the right to work, which is defended in law. The Labour Code states that "woman is entitled to equal rights with man to work and in all other relations which arise from working". Statistics reveal that women comprise almost half of the labour force and participate broadly in the economic and social life of the country; the right to free choice of profession and employment is not only recognized in the Constitution but is practised; and that there exists a rational distribution of women throughout the different sectors of employment. Women comprise 78.8 per cent of people employed in public health and the majority of those employed in education, culture, trade and State agriculture. Women make up half the workforce in the industrial sector but the percentage in transport and building is low. The percentage of women employed in every sector has risen continuously although that growth has been most substantial in industrial sectors, trade, education and culture. Within the same economic sector, however, a pattern of women's employment can be identified. Although women make up 90-95 per cent of the labour force in the textile and food industry, far fewer are employed in engineering. Similarly, while 53.8 per cent of primary teaching staff and 38.9 per cent of secondary staff are women, only 26.2 per cent of university teachers are women.

Large-scale employment of women ended their economic dependence on men and created the ground for real equality within the family and in the entire social spectrum. Rarely is the husband the only breadwinner in the family.

The law states that "equal wages be paid for equal work done, irrespective of sex, race, nationality or age". This is not a mere formality but is applied in all cases. Despite this, the average income for women is lower than that of men. A survey conducted recently among 1,700 urban families revealed that in 64.7 per cent of cases men had higher incomes than their wives; in 31.2 per cent of cases the incomes were about the same; and in only 4.1 per cent of cases did women have higher incomes than their husbands. The discrepancy between men's and women's wages occurs in part because a large number of women are employed in jobs and vocations that have low wages. This is not simply a matter of the level of schooling, as in law and practice both boys and girls have the same rights and opportunities to study at all categories of school. Approximately 75 per cent of students who complete compulsory education continue to secondary education. Of those, girls comprise 51.5 per cent (46.3 per cent at secondary vocational schools and 60 per cent at general secondary schools). They also account for 51.3 per cent of all students at university and in other forms of higher education. Women make up 47 per cent of the workforce with secondary vocational education and 37.9 per cent with university education. In 1965 only 11.9 per cent of the female workforce had higher education. In addition to professional distinctions, income differentials also arise from vocational qualifications. Despite the initial equality of access and opportunity, further vocational qualifications are difficult for women to obtain and it is those that seem to have a more direct effect on employment and income level.

One of the main reasons for the difference in vocational qualifications between men and women is connected with the home and family obligations of women. Women have little free time or opportunity to commit themselves to raising their cultural and professional level by reading and other activities. Furthermore, the transition to a higher level is usually accompanied by only a minimal increase in salary, that for many women is inadequate compensation for the effort required to gain the qualification.

Income differences also exist between rural and urban areas as well as between men and women in those areas. The average monthly income of a farmer is 7 per cent below the national average but the income of collective farmers is 36 per cent less than State farmers and 40 per cent less than the national average. The majority of employees on the collective farms are women, while men tend to be employed in State enterprises, particularly in oil and mining industries. In many rural families, men receive an income between 2 and 4 times higher than that received by women. This contributes to the persistence of strong patriarchal family relations in rural areas where 65 per cent of the Albanian population reside. A survey conducted recently in 100 rural villages revealed that in 75-78 per cent of families interviewed, the man administered the joint income of the family.

Working conditions are also of concern to Albanian workers. Outdated technology and the low level of mechanization has resulted in low productivity and long working hours. The average working week is 48 hours, or 6 eight-hour days. It is even longer in agriculture, and could be up to 12 hours per day. In several sectors of light industry, chemical industries and foodstuff there are thousands of women who work three shifts or more. Hygiene and sanitary conditions on the job are generally poor and industrial pollution is becoming an alarming problem. Health centres often function only formally due to major shortages of equipment and medicine.

For the first time since the end of the Second World War, unemployment has become a recognized problem and in proportions that are constantly increasing. Many enterprises previously subsidized by the State are closing and others, because of shortages of raw materials, cannot guarantee work for their labour force. In the State sector alone there are 32,700 unemployed people. Of those, 61 per cent are women. The number of unemployed is expected to rise further, with the highest predicted level being from 30 to 40 per cent. Women's labour will become more vulnerable in such a climate as a substantial percentage of women are employed in the non-profitable enterprises vulnerable to closure due to competition from bigger enterprises and joint-ventures financed with foreign capital. New legislation is in the process of being drafted that should ensure that the State and enterprises provide adequate financial compensation to redundant workers.

Private activities and private sectors in the economy have expanded and are creating new possibilities for employment for a proportion of the unemployed. Trade, crafts and services have opened up new opportunities for private activity. Women, particularly, have begun to explore private avenues of employment including self-employment as dressmakers, baby-sitters and day-care providers.

The rise in unemployment has also given rise to a phenomenon unknown since the 1930s: mass emigration. In the nine months following July 1990, the number of Albanian emigrants exceeded 100,000. Women and girls accounted for 10 per cent of that figure. It has been estimated that the number of people who want to leave the country, citing the difficult economic situation as the reason, is about three or four times greater. A special directorate for emigration affairs has been established to control and monitor the outflow of the population.

An important indicator of the level of emancipation of women and one of the main standards of democracy is the level of participation of women in the political and social life of a country. In this direction too past decades have witnessed a major change in women's participation. Albania had its first women deputies, or representatives in Parliament, in 1945 where the six seats held accounted for 7.3 per cent of all seats. From 1958 the percentage of women in Parliament gradually increased until in 1974, women held 33.3 per cent of seats. In 1986 this had decreased to 29.2 per cent. In the local organs of State power, such as the people's councils, women account for more than 40 per cent of their elected members, and 30 per cent of the members of the Supreme Court.

The role of women in the highest legislative organs and in the political life of the country, however, has never corresponded to the number of seats they occupy in Parliament or the local organs of State power. Special quotas have been introduced to determine women's representation, but specific selection criteria are also applied to the choice of candidate that, combined with the manner of the organization and the functioning of Parliament, have not resulted in the voice of women being properly heard at the highest levels nor in their effective role in executive State power. Policy is generally formulated on the basis of the opinions of the party leaders with women often being reminded that their rights are effectively "gifts" made by the Party, therefore not basic and inalienable.

Women's participation at the highest level of decision-making sharply declined after the election of 31 March 1991. Of the total number of proposed candidates only 9.9 per cent were women. The new Parliament had only nine women members, which amounted to 3.6 per cent of all members, and no woman held a portfolio. This was the lowest percentage of women's representation in 45 years. It has been explained by reference to the age of the new parties (the oldest being three months and the youngest barely two months), and their professed difficulties in recruiting large numbers of women into their ranks and then selecting women with the appropriate personality and skills to adequately represent them in Parliament. Undoubtedly, the number of women in Parliament will increase and they will be more effective in articulating and defending the interests of all women. Nevertheless, Albanian women still have to fight to secure a broader part in the political life of the country.

Another issue of relevance to the emancipation of women is their position within the family. Compared to all other spheres, the level of equality within the family is still low. Women devote far more time than men to housework. The majority of women (89 per cent) spend between two and four hours per day on housework whereas the majority of men (57 per cent) spend less than one hour per day. The share of household chores does not change even on holidays. The economic changes of the past few years, and in particular of the past few months, has increased that burden within the family as acute shortages of food force women to spend a great deal of their time queuing. The burden on women is more acute in rural areas where women often do not have the assistance of electrical household appliances. A survey conducted recently has revealed that although approximately 52 per cent of urban families have a washing machine only 2 per cent of rural families own one. Furthermore, only 20 per cent of rural families have indoor supplies of running water. The rest have taps outside or collect water from common taps in the village centre. Rural women are also likely to have responsibility for a larger family than their city counterparts. Whereas the average number of members in a family in urban areas is 4.6, in rural areas it is 6.4 and, in some areas, 7.8 or even 8.2. More of a woman's time is thus required to care for other people.

The burden of employment, daily housework and other family duties not only results in physical exhaustion and nervous tension among women, it also denies or restricts their access to rest, entertainment, social activities, debate and activities that would raise women's cultural and professional level. It could be argued that the unequal division of this type of work gives rise to an unequal division of free time, with women having from two to three hours less free time in their day than men. This inequitable situation can be solved by a fairer division of labour between family members as well as increased and improved goods and services, including household appliances, laundry services and packaged food products.

The economic and social transformations that have taken place in Albania have led to serious discussion about employment policy and social security conditions. The reduction of working hours and the prolongation of annual holidays are both on the agenda of WUA. Of particular importance are measures designed to assist pregnant women and young mothers. Although women are currently entitled to six months maternity leave many people are of the opinion it should be increased. Again, this has been included in the programme of all the political parties and of WUA, who is demanding that maternity leave should be increased to one to two years. Maternity benefits include paid maternity leave for six months at the rate of 80 per-cent of current wages; maternity leave is counted towards seniority for pension purposes; a woman is legally guaranteed a return to her job upon completion of maternity leave; a mother is allocated two breaks per day of 30 minutes duration each, paid as working time, to care for her child up to nine months of age; a mother is entitled to 10 days paid medical leave (60 per cent wages) every three months to care for a sick child up to the age of seven years; upon hospitalization of a child up to the age of two years, a woman has the right to remain with the child, by a doctor's recommendation, for an unlimited period of time on 60 per cent wages; and employment is guaranteed and leave taken is calculated towards seniority.

One of the most important subjects being discussed in Albania is family planning. Until fairly recently a high birth rate has been officially encouraged in family policy, stemming largely from a perceived vulnerability of the country that only a large population could protect; a high infant mortality rate; and later, a move to provide the necessary labour to revive an economy and population decimated by war. Many of those conditions have changed and Albanian family policy is being reformulated with nearly all those involved agreeing that a policy that encourages a high birth rate is no longer justifiable or viable. Family planning occupies a significant and visible place on political and social agendas. The rights of women to decide freely on the number and spacing of children including access to reliable methods of contraception and to abortion are all being discussed. WUA and other health institutions have become active in providing information on family planning as well as the health risks associated with, for example, abortions performed without medical supervision. Lack of birth control is now being viewed generally as a serious problem that requires a serious commitment to solving it. Health and family planning education are urgently required as is the provision of adequately funded and appropriate services in established health centres. The problems of family planning and the rights of women have become, more than ever, political issues. With the extension of cooperation with international organizations and other non-governmental organizations, the changes made in legislation in Albania should bring about a visible improvement in all those areas.

B. Some questions about Albanian woman today*

Albanian women have been experiencing radical changes in both their personal lives and their social activity. WUA, connected with the Party apparatus until one year ago, has been emerging as an independ-

---

* by Lavdie Ruci.

ent, pluralistic organization with a vision for the future: a vision underpinned by a new conception of the role the organization could play in the protection of the rights and freedoms of women.

During the political debate of the few months prior to the elections on 31 March 1991, two distinct viewpoints emerged. One negated the development of women and society during the last 50 years, while the other enumerated the attainments of women and society without analysing the shortcomings. The reality is different.

In the past the human rights of women have been ignored. Albanian women were considered to be less important than men and were thus expected to perform menial manual labour (in agriculture and in the home) and to bear and raise children. Heavily veiled women and girls incarcerated within the house was common in the 1930s. Women were denied the most elementary rights of speech, of employment (in 1938 only 7 per cent of women were employed) and of education (in 1938, 95 per cent of women were illiterate). Intellectual women were represented by a handful of pupils at secondary schools, by 10-15 teachers and 3-4 artists who had completed studies at the schools and conservatories of Europe. No concrete opportunities were available for women to organize or conduct independent activity for the benefit of the people. Women shouldered the double burden of social and family responsibilities and duties.

The wholesale participation of armed Albanian women in the partisan formations in addition to the material sacrifices made by women during this period resulted in the granting of legal, moral and social rights to them to participate equally in the future of Albanian society. From 1944 onwards, Albanian society was profoundly transformed, and this was reflected in the thinking of woman, who emerged as a major force in production, the arts and culture. These transformations and new directions were as follows:

(a) Mass participation in employment (women currently comprise 46.7 per cent of the overall labour force, more than 50 per cent of the workforce involved in agriculture, trade, education and culture and 78.8 per cent in the health service);

(b) Qualification for and participation in political and economic spheres;

(c) Growth of responsibilities as teacher and regulator of family life.

The ongoing democratic transformation in concepts, political ideas and legislation has brought about and will continue to bring about radical changes in the socio-economic spheres. Moreover, the electoral campaigns, the different programmes of the political parties and the results of the democratic elections have highlighted new positions and ideas about women. For example, WUA is represented by only 12 women in the new Parliament compared to 73 in the old Parliament. That figure reflects neither the social contribution nor the intellectual achievements of women. Conversely, it aroused real concern among women that they may be used by the parties as a means of propaganda . A similar regression had occurred in the different state structures, where no woman minister and few women directors are found. Despite the progress and democratization of Albanian society, women, who comprise 37.9 per cent of working people with higher qualifications and 47 per cent of working people with secondary education, are being prevented from taking up leading positions in the country, seduced by electoral promises from one to two years maternity leave and a five-day working week.

A survey conducted during March 1991 in several production enterprises and institutions at Tirana revealed that women with secondary or higher education considered the democratization process to be the basis for their further emancipation, and conversely that they would give up waged employment if their husbands received sufficiently high wages that could provide for the family. Can a woman be independent and emancipated without material income (in Albania in the majority of cases there is no other form of income beside wages)?

The democratic process and active and mass participation in politics has placed women in a different position vis-à-vis spiritual values and traditions. However, the emancipation of women, including the creation of appropriate conditions at work and in the family, does not depend solely on the will of the parties but also on the health of the economy. Albania is certainly experiencing difficulties in this area.

The new political, economic and social conditions of Albania have brought women to the crossroads. The old equilibrium and order have been destroyed and new ones have not been established. It is hoped that cooperation with Europe and women in other countries would positively influence the economic and social development of Albania and enable Albanian women to broaden their horizons by creating the necessary conditions for them to have their own say in regard to their future and the future of society.

During this period of transition, when both a Constitutional State and a structure to deal with women's affairs have yet to be created, WUA plays a definite and active role in the application of laws, defence of working women, mothers and children, fight for improvement in legislation, as well as in safeguarding the social rights of women in the family.

The problems experienced by women in the period of transition have been specific. The problems require responses that not only promote and protect women's rights and freedoms, but that also take into account two situations.

First, all parties aim to achieve economic well-being via the free market and privatization. That, as the experience of other countries of East Europe has demonstrated, would considerably increase the ranks of the unemployed. The most vulnerable to unemployment are those least qualified, of whom the majority are women. If the "fortunate" solution advocated by political forces is accepted, that is, social assistance, women deprived of economic and social activities would be confined to the home. Could this bring hope of further emancipation? WUA should aim to become an effective defender of the rights of working women as well as the advocate of better working conditions.

Secondly, mechanisms, such as social organizations and the party, which used to intervene in family life, would cease to exist. New relationships would be created between men and women, and between couples and other members of the family, in which income would exert a major influence. WUA could provide moral and material support for women who may find themselves in difficult situations. WUA should become an authentic champion of the rights of the woman in the family, on the job and in society.

The problems of Albanian society cannot be solved without the active participation of women. Irrespective of political convictions, WUA should fight to promote the independence of women, condemning every violation of their rights. Concrete and imaginative research is needed to analyse the problems facing Albanian women and to find human solutions to these problems, according to international standards.

V. BULGARIA

A. The present situation of women*

The bloodless revolution of November 1989, the beginning of the end of the totalitarian regime in Bulgaria, made possible the initiation of new social, political and economic processes. Those changes formed the foundation of a new society based on the principles of democracy and freedom and saw the development of a system of political pluralism and the separation of legislative, executive and judicial powers. Change occurred rapidly and free and democratic elections were held in June 1990. The President of Bulgaria, who cannot be a member of a political party or political organization, was elected by Parliament and nominated by the Prime Minister, and approved by Parliament. The Cabinet Ministers were chosen by the Prime Minister and approved by Parliament. The Ministers were members of different political parties. The major task of the 400 Members of Parliament was to design the New Bulgarian Constitution but other Legislative Acts were also to be devised to expedite economic and social reforms. Once the Constitution is drafted the Parliament will fix the date for new elections.

Human rights

Since November 1989 a series of measures have been taken by Parliament, the office of the President and the Government to fully implement the Human Rights Bill. These measures included, on the legislative level, the adoption of a multi-party system, freedom of speech and press, guarantee of private property, guarantee of the freedom of dissidents (an amnesty for all existing political prisoners), freedom of travel to and from Bulgaria, moratorium on capital punishment and freedom of public meetings. All these measures have been enacted by Parliament and are to be included in, among others, the new Constitution, the new Labour Code, the new Penal Code and the new Family Code.

The status of women has not been specifically targeted for change. Their status as members of the State, however, has been reconsidered and amended within the general context of changes to the political structure relating to fundamental human rights, democracy and freedom. The legislation that existed prior to November 1989 contained no clauses that discriminated against women. Since September 1944, women have had the right to vote and to stand for election and to participate in State bodies on an equal basis with men. However, de jure equality does not mean de facto equality. In spite of the many benefits that have been accorded to Bulgarian women, hidden discrimination against women persists and has been confirmed by the most recent research, which identified the existence of many inequalities in the everyday life of women. The analysis provided here is intended to show how Bulgarian women accept the reform from a centrally planned economy to a market economy; how they see their role as mothers, wives and workers during the transition period; and the lifestyle they have and would like to have.

The majority of Bulgarian women participate in the labour force. The basic guidelines for social policy relating to women, children and the family were laid down in 1973 and have given rise to a number of legislative acts that have provided increased material support to women. A significant achievement of policy was the complete equalization of labour and social rights in the case of motherhood for women working in agriculture with those employed in industry and offices. By the beginning of the Decade for Women: Equality, Development and Peace (1976-1985) Bulgaria had gone a long way towards solving the problems of women's equality, including the creation of the necessary conditions for women's full integration into social development, as evidenced by the active participation of women, and the positions they occupied, in public life. Their share in State bodies has risen steadily: 21 per cent of national Ministers of Parliament are women; 24.3 per cent of all senior executives and their deputies are women; women have gained extensive representation in the legal profession - 60.6 per cent of judges in regional courts are women, 45.7 per cent in district courts and 23.4 per cent in the Supreme Court.

The Constitution of 1971 specified in article 35 that "(1) All citizens of the People's Republic of Bulgaria are equal before the law. (2) No privileges or restrictions on rights based on nationality, origin, religion, sex, race, education, social or material status are allowed. (3) The State guarantees the equality of citizens by providing conditions and possibilities for the exercise of their rights and the fulfilment of their obligations." Article 36 stated that men and women had equal rights, while others ensured that the interests of mothers and children and marriage and the family were protected. Mothers were allowed maternity leave for pregnancy, childbirth and the raising of children. The leave began 45 days prior to birth and continued, if the mother desired, until the child was three years old. The leave was paid, in the case of the first, second and third child, until the child was two years old, then unpaid leave could be taken. The

---

*   by Raia Staikova-Alexandrova, Organizational Behavior and Management, Academy of Science.

additional leave could be used by the father or his or the mother's parents, upon agreement of the mother, and the employer could not refuse to grant such leave. If the mother returned to work after the child was two years of age, she was entitled to receive in addition to her wages half of the established cash compensation for the portion of leave not taken. Unpaid leave was calculated on the length of service. Such calculation of length of service was also extended to non-working mothers. Additional legislation defined other cases when the State granted social security payments to non-working mothers. These included university and college students, as well as women who gave birth within six months of completion of a course of study or within six months of leaving a job. The intention of those provisions was to support maternity and to encourage a three-child family model. Above all, they were designed to create the conditions necessary for ensuring women's equal rights and to promote the correct combination of women's social activity, that is, their maternal functions with their participation in the labour process and public life.

Women at work

The principle of equality between the sexes was consistently upheld in Bulgaria and the main indicator of equality was equal pay for equal work. This principle allowed no exceptions and was rigorously observed in practice. Bulgaria had ratified the 1951 International Labour Organisation Convention No. 100 concerning equality in labour. One of the basic tenets of equality in employment was the "same salary for the same work". Men and women received equal pay for work of equal value. That did not mean, however, women enjoyed equal de facto status in terms of structural and functional distribution of employment. In some branches of the economy, such as education and health, women predominated. Over time, it became accepted that professions such as teaching, medicine and dentists would be dominated by women. That situation, the feminization of professions, had a number of negative effects including a sharp reduction in the prestige of these professions. Analysis of the structure of a variety of professions by job category revealed that men and women were not equally represented. Although a comparatively equal representation of women and men was found at the lower levels, the higher up in the executive hierarchy the fewer women were found.

The 1971 Constitution embodies the principle of safe and healthy working conditions for everybody. The law upholds that right and details special requirements for the protection of particular categories of workers, among them women, who account for 50 per cent of the workforce. It is forbidden, for example, for women to perform operations that are arduous or harmful to their health and their function as mothers and, particularly for girls under 18 years of age, to work in places that involve vibrations, noise, ultrasound and VHF waves. A list that by law must be updated in accordance with changed working conditions was compiled of jobs that met such conditions and included occupations in mining and metallurgy and some activities in the printing and construction industries. The actual conditions under which women work are often quite different. Investigations undertaken in 1991 revealed that many women preferred to work under those conditions because of higher salaries (18 per cent of women surveyed); additional paid annual leave (13 per cent) and the possibility of early retirement (11 per cent). A declaration of voluntary denial of their right was usually signed by those women. The majority of women employed under those conditions are single mothers or women with family problems. The reasons women gave for preferring to work night-shifts are similar.

Pension rights also vary by sex. Women are sometimes granted a pension under more favourable conditions than men. The most widely available pension is that provided according to length of service. Women are eligible for a pension after 15 and 20 years service or 20 years service and aged 55 years whereas men are only eligible after 25 years service and aged 60.

Once private business became legal at the start of the reform period, women's economic activity expanded to include entrepreneurial activity. Approximately 600 private companies belong to women or have a woman as the president of an associated company. Of those 600, only 30 are registered in the special register for business - who's who of Bulgarian business. In 1990 women owned 1.1 per cent of companies and accounted for 5.2 per cent of the presidents of associated companies, both a slight drop compared with the figures for the previous year. Other data on that type of activity indicate that women tend to prefer to work with somebody else as responsibility is then shared. Women are not risk-takers as indicated in the absence of bankruptcies among companies owned by women. Although private business has been allowed for only two years, a number of male-owned companies have already failed.

Women's economic activity confirms the thesis that differences in value systems, aptitude and motivation exist between men and women that determine the differences in their professional behaviour. Women scientists, for example, are less likely to make their doctoral dissertation than male scientists although their performance is the same as their male colleagues according to the criteria of the scientific community. Women appeared to attach more significance to the process of attainment of professional results than to the attainment itself and at the same time need their function of mother and wife for personal satisfaction. Women obtain self-satisfaction from three different types of activity, mother, wife and worker, while men's satisfaction is rooted in their professional activity. That partly accounts for the high concentration of women at the lower levels of a professional hierarchy and their comparatively low representation among management. In the formal decision-making process women are also largely absent. Of the 400 Members of Parliament only 32, or 8 per cent, of them are women and only 1 woman is a Minister. Of the 88 leaders of political parties and organizations only 7 are women. As the process of hiring staff is still underway figures cannot be provided for the number of women employed in the various ministries.

Women in education

Education is free in Bulgaria and women are not discriminated against in access to education, except in Army schools and colleges, but that changed recently when a few women were enrolled. During the 1989/90 academic year, 48.8 per cent of students enrolled were women and 59.2 per cent of university professors were women. That had dropped from 48.9 and 64.9 per cent respectively from the 1988/89 academic year. Some of the university courses for 1990/91 were taxed. A new Educational Law was under preparation and the Parliamentary working group had invited discussion and comment from the general public. It is possible that some private education will be available next year.

Women in politics

Equal rights for women to participate in public activity are also guaranteed in the Convention on the Elimination of All Forms of Discrimination against Women, which Bulgaria has ratified. Many new political parties and organizations were established after November 1989, and of the 88 currently operating 2 are women's organizations. The Union of Democratic Unions and the Christian Democratic Movement share similar aims, which include an improvement in the real status of women in Bulgaria, a guarantee of social security and support for their members and assistance in the search for work. Again, of the leaders and their deputies of the 88 organizations only 18.6 per cent were women.

The constitutional code established in Bulgaria that is reflected in the various laws and codes, such as the Labour Code and the Family Code, form a legal system that is one of the most advanced in Europe regarding the rights of women. The system has accorded women the possibility to fully participate in the social and political life of the country.

Economic reform and the role of women

According to cultural and national traditions women are the active members in the family. They are familiar with their rights and obligations and tend to be the ones who care for the family as well as take responsibility for its functioning. Women are the ones who decide on the number of children to have, the type of education they will receive and the social contacts the family will have. Women also take care of aged parents, both theirs and their husbands. At the same time women comprise more than 50 per cent of the national labourforce and actively take part in political demonstrations and meetings. Women were more active during the period of crisis and their labourforce participation increased. The post-crisis period saw a drop in the percentage of women employed, although it did not reach the pre-crisis period. The crisis period affected women's ability to adapt to new situations and thus resulted in a group with greater flexibility towards occupational change and towards role modification. Women are more likely to change their occupations in accordance with their value system, attitudes and motivations.

Analysis of the economic and social situation during the period of transition from a centrally planned economy to a market economy reveals that a crisis has not only taken place in the economic sphere but also in the socio-psychological sphere. People were not prepared for such dramatic changes that removed all certainty of what the future held and increased the likelihood of experiencing such unknowns as unemployment. Poverty had been experienced by everyone and not widely differentiated according to social strata.

The reform changed those assumptions and brought to the surface previously hidden conflicts. The majority of workers unemployed were women, approximately 62 per cent, despite the fact that they had the same educational level as and often better qualifications than men. At the same time recent research revealed that in 45 per cent of families wives contribute more than 50 per cent to the family budget.

Unemployment is rising rapidly. In July 1990 about 30,000 people were unemployed, 19,499 of them women, but by February 1991 that figure had reached 136,000 with 62 per cent of them women. Approximately 15,000 unemployed persons hold university degrees and employment appears more difficult for them to find.

Before the reform process began and despite the excellent legal provisions preventing discrimination on the grounds of sex, hidden unemployment and hidden discrimination against women did exist. The social policy was designed to keep women at home although only 20 per cent of working women showed any desire to leave the labour force. The same result was gained in a number of surveys between 1972 and February 1991. Attitudes of family members towards unemployed women are worsening. Unemployment and lack of future security has led to increased aggressiveness among people and an increase in mental diseases and suicides.

A social policy designed to protect the social benefits enjoyed by women must be worked out and implemented during the transition period. Those benefits are in conflict with the principles of the market economy and have already begun to be eroded.

Most women desire to work outside the home and their right to choose between that or remaining at home should be safeguarded. The new economic situation renders it necessary to promote changes in the attitudes and motivations of both men and women and to set up a network of training courses to act as a barrier to social conflict, especially a set of training centres designed for women.

B. Participation of women in political life in the process of the democratization of society*

The economic, social and political changes that began in Bulgaria in late 1989 were accompanied by changed attitudes to human rights that required, in addition to legislation, new practical guarantees of their exercise. The gradual expansion of individual freedom and increased sensitivity to any violation of human rights resulted in an increased awareness and assertion of women's rights as an important dimension of human rights. It was recognized that although socialist society had provided guarantees of a wide variety of political, economic, social and cultural rights, they had also devised a complex and rigid system that effectively suppressed the exercise of those rights. Women were most adversely affected by that system as, according to socialist theory, they were required to be mothers, workers, "front-rankers in socialist production", public activists, housewives and wives at the expense of personal, professional and public self-fulfilment. The grave economic situation and the process of economic reform, however, has posed serious difficulties to guarantees of the exercise of newly acquired social rights, particularly those of women, and has led to questions of women's role and place in society.

Equality between men and women is a problem faced by all modern societies. Bulgaria has a long-standing tradition of formal equality between men and women that is enshrined in the Turnova Constitution of the Bulgarian Principality, in the two Constitutions of 1947 and 1971 and in a number of additional laws that provide juridical guarantees of equality. De jure equality notwithstanding, the general situation and status of women is lower than that of men. The percentage of women who are elected to the National Assembly (the Bulgarian Parliament) or who held senior positions in the State or Government has been traditionally low. Women's participation in the country's political, social and economic life is minimal particularly when compared with their role in society. The majority of working women also hold unskilled and underpaid jobs and are more likely to lose their jobs in the period of growing unemployment.

Would the mere enactment of appropriate legislation guarantee women equal rights with men? The enactment of such laws and legislation has moral rather than practical value in that it expresses an official State policy that prohibits discrimination on the basis of sex and regards men and women as equal before the law and within society. Laws are easier to change than traditions and attitudes that are deeply rooted in the consciousness of the society. To look to the law as an indicator of equality may be misleading, the real status of women within society and the family can only be determined by the extent of their equality within the socio-economic sphere, labour and the social security system. Women's biological function requires special legislation to protect both her labour and her maternity and thus renders her unequal with men. The concessions that women enjoy are at variance with the demand for equality. Anti-discrimination legislation eliminated the direct forms of discrimination against women but could not eliminate their actual inequality with men, which is economically determined.

The background of economic crisis has highlighted inequality in women's economic situation. Women are more vulnerable to unemployment but at the same time are forced to perform better on the labour market in order to increase their income to satisfy their needs. In addition to employment, women spend the majority of their time shopping, caring for children and doing housework. Such conditions do not leave women much time let alone desire to become involved in political and public life. The political and economic reform under way in Bulgaria has led to an increased conservatism among women that is reflected in the percentage of women who support the Bulgarian Socialist Party, the successor to the communist party, and disapprove of the Union of Democratic Forces, an opposition group. Similarly,

* by Verginia Veltcheva, Legal Adviser, Office of the President.

according to a recent public opinion poll, women are far less likely than men to voice a political preference. Women's participation in political life is minimal, limited in scope and largely occurs through existing political organizations and parties. Women's representation among the leadership of those groups is insignificant.

Prior to the recent free elections, women's representation in the Bulgarian Parliament was determined by an artificially fixed quota that varied between 20 and 23 per cent. After the elections in June 1990, the sharp political polarization gave rise to nominees being judged on political affiliation rather than personal merit. Women's representation in the new Bulgarian Parliament has dropped dramatically to less than 8 per cent. The representation of women in the Grand National Assembly, however, could be said to mirror their participation in political life. Of the 400 parliamentarians, only 34 are women, of whom 24 belong to the Bulgarian Socialist Party, 9 to the Union of Democratic Forces and 1 to the Bulgarian Agrarian Party. Women parliamentarians have been elected to lead seven parliamentary committees. Despite the new criteria, the number of women who held highly placed positions in State Government did not drop.

Another problem, relevant to the involvement of women in public and political life, is that of how society judges that involvement. Results from periodic public opinion polls suggest that women politicians have greater difficulty in gaining the electorates recognition and would more easily lose that recognition than men. Furthermore, the popularity of women politicians has declined despite their prominent political endeavours.

The new free conditions of association that have prevailed in Bulgaria since 1989 have not led to the formation of a universal organization of women designed to represent their specific interests and rights. The Democratic Union of Women, which replaced the women's organization that existed within the State-controlled Fatherland Front, an umbrella organization composed of existing political parties and organizations, is ideologically and functionally connected with the Bulgarian Socialist Party. The Nadezhda (Hope) Democratic Movement of Women is local and its activities are largely confined to fund-raising and relief work. Women's social and economic interests are defended by two trade unions: the Confederation of Independent Trade Unions in Bulgaria and the Podkrepa Confederation of Labour.

The considerable changes that have occurred in Bulgaria over the 18 months have not resulted in any radical change in the position of women. The economic crisis has made it extremely difficult to maintain their economic and social rights, but women have greater freedom now. Their involvement in political life, State government and economic reform is considered the only way that their interests may be defended, their equality maintained and their potential as women realized.

VI. BYELORUSSIAN SOVIET SOCIALIST REPUBLIC

The social and economic status of women*

The inequitable position of women in the Byelorussian Soviet Socialist Republic can be explained by reference to enduring traditional stereotypes of women's roles and ineffective government policy and decisions regulating women's status. This has been exacerbated during the current social crisis engendered by the radical social and political reforms transforming Byelorussian society. Women are bearing the brunt of these changes as they generally comprise the most unprotected stratum of society.

The status of women is determined by their access to, and equal opportunities within, education. Opportunities should also exist for young people, both male and female, to develop further professional skills in technical schools, colleges and institutions of higher education. However, in a socialist society, it had been the position of the parents in the social hierarchy and not the gender of the child that has determined access to education.

Of those having access to specialized secondary and higher education in Byelorussia, 62 per cent are women and they account for 53 per cent of the total labour force. Yet the positions they occupy in the labour force belie the achievements they have gained in the education system. Difficult, uncreative and unskilled work accounts for 40 and 70 per cent of the work in industry and agriculture, respectively, the bulk of which is performed by women. In addition, a significant number of women work under conditions that could be described as hazardous. In 1988, Byelorussian industry granted hazardous work compensation and benefits to 178,000 women who accounted for 45 per cent of all working women and 44 per cent of the total labour force. The proportion was particularly high in the chemical and petroleum industries, the building-materials industry, and the publishing and wood-processing industries. Given the child-bearing and child-rearing functions of women this could be seen to have potential as well as actual damaging effects on society. Unfortunately the situation has not changed and, where legislation exists to regulate working conditions, it is largely ignored. For example, the quota for loads a woman can move during a single shift was set at seven tonnes, far above European norms, but even that is often ignored.

One important trend observed was the increasing number of women employed in shift and night-shift positions. Women evidently wish or need to regulate their working hours to enable them to devote more time to household chores.

Perestroika and *glasnost* unveiled part of the truth about the working conditions of women in industry and agriculture but the knowledge had not changed anything. Working conditions are not improving because neither the State nor enterprises nor women themselves are interested. The State appears to have neither the will nor the desire to improve working conditions despite economic and social changes. The traditional productive goal of the fulfilment of targets above everything else is still in place with scant attention paid to working conditions except insofar as compensation for them is used to attract labour.

Ironically, the workers themselves, those apparently with the most to gain from improved working conditions appear uninterested in pursuing them. Given the difficult material conditions under which workers in Byelorussia live, it is not really surprising that workers choose the material benefits that accrue to them as compensation for the hazardous conditions under which they work rather than better conditions with lower wages. Women are particularly vulnerable to this way of thinking as they assume major responsibility within the family for caring for children and the elderly.

It could be stated that in the game of universal irresponsibility women have to assume the role of the last player "who has no one to whom to pass the ball". In such circumstances, women are willing to work under any conditions in order to earn an extra 10-rouble note or snatch an opportunity to buy something that is in short supply. But in the final analysis this "fast passing" results in a loss of health by both mother and child.

The principle of equal pay for equal work is violated constantly and everywhere, since it is the place in the hierarchy rather than product of the work that defines wages and other benefits. A comparison between workers in the same occupations and with the skill levels would reveal no difference, but if the aggregate incomes of ordinary workers and managerial staff were compared, major differences would be observed. Women are infrequent among managers and the proportion declines the higher up the hierarchy of leadership (where the percentage of women is only 5.8). This is particularly true in the management of State and collective farms.

---

*   by Lyudmila Gryaznova, Chair, Department of Political Economy, Byelorussian University.

The lack of sharing of household activities affects women's social and economic status. Estimates of the Byelorussian SSR Institute of Economics show that women spend 27.2 hours per week on average on household activities, compared with 11.4 hours for men.[1] This makes housework a second job that affects women's capacity to work in remunerated production and to organize their free time. For example, a woman in the city can allot only 17 minutes on a weekday to read newspapers, magazines or fiction, compared to only 5 minutes in the countryside and only 6 minutes and 1 minute, respectively, are left for education and skill development.[2]

The role of women in political life is similar to that in the economy. Politics in the administrative system is not a form of organized struggle and accommodation of interests of different social groups. Rather it is a form of organized repression by the party and the government apparatus against society. It is clothed in democratic apparel when many workers, collective farmers, women and youth are elected to the Byelorussian Supreme Soviet merely to endorse decisions approved by the *apparat*. The number of women elected shows nothing about their real role in politics.

Perestroika and *glasnost* revealed the truth about the nature of policy-making and permitted women to enter politics. One of the first manifestations was women's keen interest in political publications, where a poll showed that women have begun to prefer to read newspapers and magazines rather than fiction.[3] This encounter with improved information, rather than leading to efforts to control the legislature and administration has led instead to a reaction by women to the existing political regime in the form of a passive mistrust of all power structures.

Only 11 women were elected to the new Republic Parliament. A main reason was that women have had less opportunities for professional political development. Women's workload at work and at home averages 70 hours a week and will not let them achieve effective results in either field. Therefore there is no reason for women to lament that they are being discriminated against. Women will have to prove that they can be politicians, be familiar with problems of the society and find effective political ways to solve them. As the Union of Soviet Socialist Republic People's Deputy, Galina Starovoitova, put

it, women's gender ("gender" or *pol* in Russian also means "floor") should not be their ceiling.

A female politician should not only promote women's interest, but should advocate democratic changes. Compared with other countries, there are no purely women's problems, but rather general social problems accumulated during the years of the authoritarian bureaucratic regime under which all groups were subordinated. The objective of current efforts is to produce a smooth and evolutionary change to a democratic political structure without social upheavals. Under those conditions, voters do not particularly care about the gender of a candidate for Parliament, but rather elect those they feel can bring about the desired change.

One consequence of the past regime has been to develop a stereotype of behaviour in which human beings are turned into parts of a machine as the State engulfs society and the *apparat* the State. The "fatherly" care of the upper circles of the State has produced a submissive and dependent mentality among the people, which has made them capable of begging but incapable of critical and creative approaches to problems.

This mentality also characterizes women and their organizations. For example, most letters to women's magazines contain complaints and requests for assistance. The traditional women's organizations themselves cannot respond to these needs because they can only respond locally to local problems. Included in changes being made is the formation of a Committee on Women, Family, Mother and Child Protection, which represents the first time a committee to deal with the problems of women and the family has been formed at the government level. That Committee brought about the adoption in 1990 by the Supreme Soviet of the State, the Programme concerning Immediate Actions to Improve the Status of Women, Protect Mothers and Children and to Strengthen the Family. It is based on increases of benefits to be paid to certain categories of women and families, but does not deal with the kinds of investments that would eliminate the reasons for the problems the Programme is designed to solve.

In Byelorussia a department to deal with the problems of women and the family was established in 1990. It has been accumulating information on the

---

[1] BSSR Academy of Sciences, Institute of Economics, *Propositions to improve the social status of women, to strengthen the family and to protect mother and child*, No. 43/100-64 of 20.8.89, p. 40.

[2] BSSR Academy of Sciences, Institute of Economics, *Women in the Byelorussian S.S.R. 1990: Statistical digest*, Minsk, 1990, p. 98.

[3] "Women about themselves", PABOTHNUA Magazine, 1990, No. 11, p. 7.

status of women and children in the Republic. The creation of this central data bank on the status of women and the family is important because previously the information had been dispersed among different agencies such as the State Committee on Labour and Wages, the State Committee on Education, the Ministry of Health and others. The potential of this new department would be stronger if it established effective cooperation with the scientific community. Unfortunately, Byelorussia's capability in women's studies is weak because few people study the problems and then usually within the context of other social problems. Moreover, women's studies, like other social sciences, exhibit biases.

In addition to new organizations established by legislative and administrative authorities, a number of non-governmental women's organizations have sprung up recently. Women's groups appeared within the Byelorussian SSR Union of Writers and the Union of Cinema Workers. Indeed, women involved in the creative process were among the first to perceive the necessity to protect their rights and interests.

In Byelorussia, however, many social problems have become secondary because of the results of the Chernobyl accident, about which the population of the Republic, particularly in the affected areas, shows a major concern. The health of her child is what troubles the heart and soul of a woman today. In other republics it may be nationalism, the struggle of democratic and conservative forces in the course of *perestroika* or the food situation that have become acute problems that are tearing apart the social fabric. With Byelorussians, it is their common plight - Chernobyl - that unites everyone: Russians and Byelorussians, conservatives and democrats.

The dimensions of the problem have been clearly diagnosed in terms of the state of health of people in the Republic based on scientific research. The data testify to a serious deterioration in the health of the Republic's population affected by the radiation from the Chernobyl nuclear power plant accident. These results only became visible several years after the accident. The Byelorussian non-governmental women's organizations are seeking to deal with the problems on a priority basis. The newly created Organizing Committee of the Byelorussian League of Women considers the protection of women, children and youth from the consequences of the disaster to be a main aim of its activities.

This organization has been found necessary despite the existence of a government programme of assistance to the affected. As often happens, that programme exists but its implementation mechanism does not work. Thus the non-governmental grass-roots organizations provide a stimulus for the government bodies to work.

Small-scale business should become an important direction for the activities of non-governmental women's organizations, providing an outlet for the free market aspirations of women, on the one hand, and a means of social assistance to women and children, on the other. These activities, however, have not been developed by the women's organizations. In contrast to other areas, particularly larger cities in other republics, the favourable moment was missed in Byelorussia. With the passage of more rigid laws on cooperative activities and joint ventures, chances for the development of small-scale businesses have sharply decreased.

As non-governmental women's organizations grow, there will be a need for coordination of their activities. An information centre should be formed that would provide information on their activities and produce recommendations on effective ways to achieve their goals. In addition, women's organizations should work together to bring pressure to bear on legislative and administrative bodies of the State.

VII. CZECHOSLOVAKIA

A. A brief survey of the situation of Czechoslovak women at the beginning of the transitional period from a centrally planned to a market economy*

For the reforms in Eastern Europe to be successful a radically different path from that of the previous totalitarian regime has to be chosen. Economic, social, political and cultural thinking has to be completely reconstructed with the aid of new ideas, knowledge and skills. Most importantly, a redefinition of attitudes towards individual rights and responsibilities, the family, women, the community and society as a whole have to be undertaken. The intention of this paper is to highlight some of the major issues affecting women, one of the most vulnerable sectors of Czechoslovak society.

Basic demographic data

In 1980 the population of Czechoslovakia was 15,579,000 of which 7,979,000, or a little over half, were women. The population was characterized by a high mortality rate of medium age groups, a relatively high birth rate and infant mortality rate, and a high marriage rate. The two-child family was the norm. The mean life-expectancy at birth was 67 years for men and 74 years for women. Cohabitation, as opposed to marriage, was steadily increasing, particularly among younger groups. The divorce rate matched the European average and was highest among the 20-24 year age group. The number of single parent families with dependent children, the majority headed by women, was increasing. Divorce, increasing number of unmarried mothers and decreasing remarriage rates for women accounted for this. Abortion rates were among the highest in Europe, births outside of marriage were low but the number of pregnant brides, particularly in the 18-19 year age group, was very high. The latter trend was affecting the proportion of women entering employment at that age, as well as the entire structure of female unemployment as those marriages tended to be unstable and dissolved within four years.

Human rights and legal equality

The principle of equality of men and women was recognized in law: the Constitution, the Labour Code, the Family Act and social security laws enshrined it, but the practices and programmes of education and employment fell far short of this goal. De jure equality did not equal de facto equality. Of the total number of secondary school students in 1988/89, 64.5 per cent were girls but they accounted for only 40.5 per cent of those training for manual

occupations and 43.3 per cent of those attending universities. Traditional attitudes towards women and family obligations persisted and have generally resulted in the unilateral assignment of responsibility for parenting to women. But women also had one of the highest employment rates in Europe. That combination of family and employment responsibilities increased the burdens on women, and the family was often subject to additional strains, resulting in delinquency and criminality among children and juveniles.

It was essential, during the transitional period, that women and mothers should be protected by additional legislation. Such legal provisions, supported by the State, should include guaranteed economic measures aimed at pregnant women and mothers, educational programmes designed to promote sharing of parental and family responsibilities equally between men and women, legal provisions to gradually eliminate female branches of industry and comprehensive public information programmes about the problems of working women.

Social policy and child care

The 9.7 per cent rise in the number of women in the labour force between 1970 and 1980 necessitated increased social security and mother-and-child welfare services to working mothers. Those included the extension of maternity leave to three years and the payment of sickness benefits to a working parent who was required to take time off to nurse a sick child, and that sick leave counted as time worked for pension benefits. Financial support provided to pregnant women and families took a variety of forms. Compensation in the form of a levelling-out allowance could be claimed by a pregnant worker in the event of loss of income during her pregnancy due to transference, on the grounds of health, to a lower paying position. At the birth of a child a mother was paid a birth-grant to assist in the purchasing of a layette and other essential items. Maternity benefits were payable during maternity leave for a period of 28 weeks or 37 weeks for single mothers and mothers of twins. That benefit could be drawn by the father in the event of hospitalization, illness or death of the mother.

A family allowance was payable for all children of school age or up to the age of 26 for completion of professional training. The allowance increased with

---

* by Ludmila Venerova, Adviser to the Prime Minister's Office.

the number of children. Also payable, since October 1990, was the new parental allowance that was paid to either parent, at the conclusion of the maternity benefit, providing full-time at-home care for a child under the age of three. Parents could also alternate in their care of the child. During the sickness of a child, one employed parent could claim a family nursing benefit, provided under health insurance, which was payable for a period not exceeding 7 days per illness, and 13 working days for a single-parent family.

Young couples were eligible to apply for a loan to newly-weds, which was repayable over a period of 15 years at a very low interest rate. At the birth of their first child and for subsequent children a portion of that loan was written off the debt as a State grant. Families in financial difficulties could apply for social welfare assistance, which was provided in the form of a lump-sum payment or as an alimentation allowance for children. Those were payable according to a nationally determined social minimum that differed with the age of a child. Special benefits were payable to foster parents and to the families of soldiers on National Service duty. Finally, tax relief on wages was provided to the parent drawing the family allowance. Many of those allowances were drawn from the health-insurance system, but with the change to a market economy and the emergence of new forms of employment as well as rising unemployment, it was expected that those will form part of a system of State-paid benefits.

Inadequate responsible parenthood and family-planning education, comprehensive social security for very young families and insufficient knowledge and use of contraceptive devices have contributed to Czechoslovakia having one of the lowest average age of women at the birth of their first child in Europe, but also an inordinately high rate of abortions. Family planning is therefore of particular concern. Responsible approaches to conception as well as improved birth-control methods are urgently needed. Comprehensive health education should also be introduced into schools and should form part of parental child care. This is particularly important as the physical environmental deteriorates and children's health remains poor, with a significant number suffering from obesity, due to insufficient physical activity, and inflammation of the upper air passages and asthma.

According to surveys, childcare formed the main activity of parents in Czechoslovak homes. Although social security regulations provide for both parents, the responsibility for such care generally rests with the mother. The high labour-force participation rate of women requires the State to provide alternative care in pre-schools and kindergartens, but the recent introduction of parental allowance led to a substantial fall in the need for nurseries. Despite that and the financial assistance provided to families, women still assume major responsibility for the well-being of the

family and a full-time employed woman spends another 9.5-10 hours per day travelling to and from work and shopping for household needs. That, in addition to household tasks, has a negative effect on family relations, women's health and professional activities. The framework of State family policy should change to allow families greater freedom to decide on the type of assistance required to maintain the health and standard of living of the family.

Poverty is increasing in Czechoslovakia as indicated by increased claims for social-care benefits. A recent survey estimates that approximately 4.5 per cent of families with dependent children and 9 per cent of pensioners are living below the poverty line. Ethnic minorities are also at high risk of poverty. In 1989, 8.2 per cent of the net national income of Czechoslovakia was spent on social assistance to families with dependant children, not including expenditure on education, health and culture. In view of the social problems expected to occur as a result of the transition from a centrally planned economy to a market economy a social safety net is required to prevent people slipping into a permanent state of poverty. This net should establish a baseline below which families could not be expected to manage and should thus be compensated with a range of benefits and services to maintain a guaranteed minimum income.

Employment of women

Given that the average living standards for a family in Czechoslovakia can practically be maintained only when both partners work, it is not surprising that women's share of the labour force approaches 50 per cent. Women can expect to work from the completion of their occupational training or education until the retirement age of 55 years, with breaks for child rearing. An examination of the labour-force participation rates for 1970 and 1980 according to age reveals similar changes for both men and women. The participation rate of the 15-24 years age group and the 40-49 years age group decreased while that of 25-39 years group increased. The rate for 50-54 years age group also increased as did that for 65-69 years, but for 55-64 years it decreased. These figures reflect changed educational objectives and fertility patterns but also participation in compulsory military training and increased living costs reflected in rising economic activity, particularly among older workers whose pension benefits are proving inadequate. Older women workers are also returning to or continuing to work for companionship.

The total number of hours that may be worked in a week is regulated by law although in practice this is rarely enforced. The total working hours are generally longer than in other industrialized countries. The average normative number of working hours per week is 40.3 but the average real number of working hours is 41.9. In 1989, the percentage of women working part-time was 11.6, but 23-27 per cent of women workers would have preferred to work part-time. Since 1989, approximately 40 per cent of women workers, mostly mothers of young children, work flexible hours. Roughly 40,000 women return to work from maternity leave each year. During maternity leave they have been recorded as employed on the grounds that they have retained a claim on their job during the period of absence. Of these returning workers, 40 per cent would prefer part-time work.

Almost half of all female workers are employed in the service industry. One third are employed in industry and one fifth in agriculture. The employment of women in production had increased by 10.3 points in the past 10 years. Regulations governing women's employment ban women from performing certain jobs that are defined as physically or mentally too taxing. Those strictures together with the division of industry into light and heavy contribute to the dominance of women in certain industries, mainly those defined as light, such as clothing (89.3 per cent women) and textile (74.4 per cent women). However, the women's proportion of the work force in those industries where their participation should be minimal was actually quite high. That arose partly from the priority that had been given to heavy industry in the past, including priority for workers.

The traditionally female industries are not without their problems. Over the years they have suffered from a lack of resources with which technological improvements could have been made and thus working conditions improved. Shift work is far more common in these industries, with one in three women in Czechoslovakia working shifts. In 1987, 8.7 per cent of women employed in those industries worked under conditions hazardous to their health, the most frequent being noise followed by the handling of chemical substances. Of this work-force, 10-12 per cent performed jobs characterized as constant, intensive and monotonous, and requiring little skill.

The high percentage of female labour employed in those industries could cause difficulties for employers, particularly if those employed are young mothers who frequently require time off, for example, to nurse a sick child. Employers would then have to rely on women of retirement age or those returning to work after retirement for completion of production assignments.

Women and men's employment is also spread across a number of occupations assessed as suitable jobs for women and jobs for men. That division is not only because of the traditional assessment of women's ability to perform certain activities, such as nurses and carers, it is also due to better opportunities for arranging working hours compatible with family duties and responsibilities, that is, for securing shorter

working hours and longer vacations (teachers), flexible working hours (health service) and irregular working hours (social welfare). The majority of women workers could be classified as white-collar workers and dominate such occupations as teaching and nursing, and occupations within the catering and health and welfare industries. Moreover, although the percentage of jobs held by women that require secondary or university education has increased, only 69 per cent of women are employed according to their qualifications and 15 per cent are performing substantially less skilled work than they were trained for. Child-rearing appears to be the major reason for this as women choose convenience over appropriateness when selecting a job. That is particularly apparent in single-parent families where 21.5 per cent of mothers hold jobs for which they are overqualified.

The collection of gender-disaggregated statistics is a basic requirement for implementing the tasks set forth in the Nairobi Forward-looking Strategies. As employment status statistics are not collected this way, economic and sociological surveys have been the only source of data from which to obtain such information. Those reveal that length of practice, organizational ability, personal ambition and educational attainment are the important factors in determining type and level of employment. One survey reveals that not quite one third of all employed women have ambitions to hold managerial posts. Of the total female labour force, 14 per cent hold managerial positions, 25 per cent of those in middle-level management and only 10 per cent in senior management. In 1987, 12.7 per cent of women held political office and 51.3 per cent of all working women had functioned in voluntary organizations. In the first free elections held in Czechoslovakia in 1990, 21 per cent of the members elected to the Federal Assembly and 17 per cent of those elected to the local authorities were women. Only one woman minister is in the Czechoslovak Federal Government, one in the Czech Government and none in the Slovak Government. In general, the percentage of women who hold senior posts is substantially lower than indicated by their educational attainment and length of practical experience. Only a small proportion of women in the younger and middle-age groups, however, can acquire the necessary additional education to further their professional development, largely due to their responsibility for bearing and rearing children. The critical factor in women's professional advancement is thus the presence or absence of children. The largest percentage of women managers occurs in the 50-55 years age group, that is, when child-rearing is largely complete and women are free to devote time to professional development.

Women's earnings

Despite proclamations of just remuneration according to the value of work accomplished, policies on wages have tended to value physically strenuous labour over mental effort. In 1984 and 1988, a survey was carried out of the earnings of men and women. The results of both showed that the earnings of women were lower throughout their lives than those of men. In 1984 the average female wage was 68.9 per cent of that of men and in 1988, 70.9 per cent. Age and educational attainment had an effect on this difference. The difference between the wages of men and women was least for university graduates entering employment. From 30 years of age there was an increasing difference between the monthly earnings of men and women, with those of women lagging behind by one third. While men's salaries grew fastest between the ages of 30 and 40, women's salaries rose fastest after 35, but that rise was substantially smaller. At retirement, women's earnings averaged three quarters of those of men and thus further disadvantaged them in the computation of the old-age pension. Despite the slight advantage in wages of university-trained women, throughout the course of a woman's working life her income did not reach the level of a man's regardless of educational attainment.

The lower average earnings of women are due to a number of factors. The concurrent maternal and professional obligations of women disadvantage them in the labour force. The persistence of traditional attitudes to the roles and obligations of men and women mean an insufficient sharing of parental responsibilities, with women assuming the bulk of the associated duties at the expense of career development. Both social security provisions and family law contribute to the double burden of women as they also strongly link women with children. The persistent undervaluing of women's work, underestimation of the social significance of child-raising and ignorance of the generally high occupational and educational standards of women create a special labour category that continually loses out to men.

The transition to a market economy also saw the rise of a new phenomenon for Czechoslovakia: unemployment. Although the unemployment rate is extremely low, 1.5 per cent in January 1991, it is nevertheless expected to have an impact on employment patterns and living standards, particularly those of women. The ratio of unemployed women to men is as yet unknown but it is expected that women will, by virtue of type and location of employment, become increasingly disadvantaged in the labour market compared with men. Unemployment assistance, including the payment of benefits, employment search and retraining schemes, is being introduced but it is expected that women will again be worse off than men financially as the benefit paid will represent a percentage of the average monthly wage of the last employment period.

Women's organizations

Women's representation in decision-making positions is very low. With the abolishment of the Czechoslovak Council of Women after the "Velvet Revolution", the role of the remaining 40 or so different councils and committees of women has become more important. Although the women's movement has yet to define its goal it is expected to establish a council for equal status in the near future to complete the tasks set out in the Nairobi Forward-looking Strategies.

New trends emerging from the recent political changes

The general democratization underway in Czechoslovakia should in due course bring about a rise in the percentage of women represented in top management. However, for that to occur a number of stringent measures will be required that may prove unpopular with women. New family policy will require families to take more responsibility for their own lives, which will increase the scope of activity, freedom and decision-making within families. Economic reform will involve liberalization of prices, taxation changes, economization of housing and energy and privatization, all of which may contribute to a decrease in real income, consumption and thus in living standards. The number of children living in poverty may treble. Unemployment among vulnerable groups, such as Gypsies, is expected to be particularly high. Charitable organizations and the Church will probably be required to provide more assistance to more people in need but the State should provide financial assistance for such activity. Substantial help from abroad cannot be relied upon due to a drop in world economic prosperity. The environment also requires immediate and expensive attention if further damage is to be prevented. The inability of people to quickly adapt to dramatic changes in society is leading to social tension that must be resolved before full and active participation in the changes can be expected. The application of democratic principles in management and in social life, carrying out economic reform aimed at increased efficiency of the Czechoslovak economy, and concurrent social reform based on principles of personal responsibility combined with a State-provided social safety net, are the most urgent tasks of the present and of the near future.

B. The influence of social and economic changes in the Czech and Slovak Federal Republic on the position of women*

Equal positions of men and women

The process of change in Czechoslovakia is not yet complete particularly in terms of legislation. The proposed new draft Constitution stresses the concept of liberty and extends the rights and freedoms of citizens. It guarantees equal rights and duties of citizens, regardless of nationality, race or sex. Men and women are guaranteed equality in the family, employment and public activities. The Constitution accords with the articles of the Convention on the Elimination of All Forms of Discrimination against Women. However, as the old Constitution is not always observed, particularly regarding equality of men and women in work and freedom of expression, an evaluation of the application of the new Constitution would only be possible once it was passed. Many new bills have been recently passed by the Federal Assembly and the legislation generally did not discriminate against women. Difficulties arose, however, when the de jure and de facto situations of women were compared.

Economic reforms and women's economic participation

According to the Labour Code, amended in 1990, all citizens of Czechoslovakia have an equal right to work, to freely choose an occupation, to just and satisfactory working conditions, to protection against unemployment and to the receipt of wages. During the preceding regime, the right to work established the basis for women's emancipation. In 1948, approximately one third of women were employed; today 46 per cent of all workers are women. Women are also legally guaranteed equality of access to education. Education is of a good quality and women represent 64.7 per cent of students at secondary vocation schools, 40.5 per cent at apprentice schools and 45 per cent of those enrolled at universities. Women's high level of education and participation in the labour force is not, however, reflected in their occupation of managerial posts. Due largely to family responsibilities, women prefer less responsible, less time-consuming occupations that are generally not commensurate with their qualifications. That contributes to the large difference observed between the wages of women and men. On average women earned 40 per cent less than men. Shortened working hours for women, assignment of women to more demanding labour posts and the shortcomings in the application of wage regulations all have a negative effect on women's wages. Women's wages also tend to remain stable, not attracting the periodic

rises related to economic growth. Research indicates that women's wages are considered to be largely supplementary to family income or a form of "social help".

The first half of 1990 saw a decrease of 1.3 per cent in the number of employees. Although this figure was not broken down by gender, an examination of the distribution of unemployment reveals a large decrease in the number of employees in sectors dominated by women. That ranged from a 1.1 per cent decrease in culture to 2.2 per cent in industry. In addition, an increasing number of women are working reduced hours. Since the end of the 1980s, there has been a tendency for the number of women working part-time to increase. This tends to mask the employment situation of women and, indeed, statistics on the phenomenon are from research studies rather than official statistics. In 1987, 8.1 per cent of women were working fewer hours per week and three years later that percentage had increased to 11.6. In contrast, although official figures suggest a decrease, studies suggest that women's overtime work has remained the same, at an average of 47.4 hours per year. This is largely due to low productivity, outmoded equipment and shortages of labour in unattractive branches of the economy, as well as to the need for higher incomes. Nightwork, however, has been decreasing. Women are also more likely to work under hazardous conditions.

Unemployment is beginning to be women's greatest problem, as a result of economic reform and price liberalization. Most families remain dependent on the incomes of both spouses and there are a large number of households where the woman is the only income-carner.

New forms of employment for women are beginning to appear but that appearance has been hampered by legislative regulations, particularly those governing the payment of taxes. In one case an association of women entrepreneurs and managers provide a consulting and education service for women.

Participation in the decision-making process

After the 1986 elections, 29.4 per cent of representatives in the Federal Assembly, 30 per cent of the Slovak National Council and about 40 per cent in trade unions were women. That form of constitutional equality is not extended to managerial functions, however, where "the lower the function the more women" appears to be the rule. Similarly, although

---

*   by Anna Okruhlicova, Women's International Democratic Federation.

key decision-making organs receive proposals by women those largely remain "for discussion" and render women's participation notional rather than actual. In 1990, women's share in those decision-making structures fell to 10 per cent in the Federal Assembly and 11 per cent in the Slovak National Council. There are no women representatives in the Slovak Government and only one each in the Federal Government and the Czech Government. Women comprise only 19 per cent of the higher posts in local administration. The Governmental Committee for Woman and Family, an advisory body established by the Slovak Government in 1990, is not operating.

The drop in women's representation can be explained partly by the reduced number of women candidates listed by political parties. Traditional attitudes towards women's maternal duties also influence the level of women's participation in decision-making. The problem is complicated by past experiences and expectations of the working environment and requires major changes in habits and attitudes that may take a generation to accomplish.

Parental and household duties of women

Parental rights and duties were established in Family Law, which has not yet been amended. Those legal precepts were in accordance with the Convention on the Elimination of All Forms of Discrimination against Women. The marriage rate is high but divorce is increasing. That may soon be as high as one in two

in places such as Prague. The present birth-rate is the lowest in the history of the State but exceeds the European average. The rate is expected to continue to decrease due to the high cost of living. The rate of abortions is very high and has been growing since a liberal Abortion Act was passed in 1987. Last year the number of abortions performed approached the number of children born. Amendment of the Abortion Act, which is under discussion, concerns many women as it has been proposed to limit access to methods of artificial interruption of pregnancy.

The average life expectancy for men is 67.2 years and 75.6 years for women. Combined with the high divorce rate, those factors contribute to the existence of a large number of single-income families with minimal financial reserves. State social support for such families is extremely limited due to economic difficulties. For the same reason, comprehensive health care, including medical and contraceptive assistance, is not provided. The rising price of foodstuffs is proving especially difficult for young families and threatens compliance with article 12 (paragraph 2) of the Convention. According to a survey in March 1991, 11 per cent of households in Slovakia had an income insufficient to cover their needs and 44 per cent lived from salary to salary. Due to increased energy and rent costs, prices are expected to increase even further. Although the Government has made many provisions to assist the weaker sector of society, economic difficulties are rendering these measures inadequate.

VIII. HUNGARY

A. Women in the transition to a market economy[*]

Attempting to outline the positive and negative effects of the economic changes in Hungary, even though the changes that are deemed necessary to implement a market economy are still being debated, is extremely difficult. However, difficult and uncertain issues of economic transformation may be, they should be addressed and concomitant social changes examined or projected. The economy of Hungary is in a state of flux. It is in transition to a market-type economy that will itself be at stake if society is not prepared for both positive and negative consequences. The earlier those are envisaged the better the chances for developing social institutions to support them. In this paper areas are identified where special measures may be needed to assist women adjust and participate in the transformation process. For that purpose the paper focuses on current developments only. Thus the key features of women's employment are taken as granted and are not detailed, such as:

(a) The economic activity of women has traditionally been as high as that of men;

(b) The high participation rate of women has coexisted with their full-time employment, which has made their working and private life equally hard;

(c) The labour market has been highly segregated by sex: women and men have tended to find jobs in different industries (horizontal segregation) and been able to possess various posts in the hierarchy (vertical segregation).

The paper outlines possible effects on women of the economic transformation and considers a number of economic and social factors that are likely to considerably influence women's employment in the future.

Gloomy perspectives for women

At the very start of the fundamental economic and political changes it was a shared assumption among the few researchers dealing with women's issues that women would be likely to suffer disproportionately more than men during the transition process. Some even argued that women's position would be worse than under socialism. Some assumptions are based on the negative effects of economic stagnation in the second half of the 1980s, when declining living standards meant steadily increasing burdens for women. Other arguments concerned

recessions and structural changes of industrialized countries in the period 1970-1980 when women often bore the brunt of adjustment. Thus, the pessimistic views on women's prospects were based on historical and economic projections of situations completely unlike the current transition from a centrally planned economy to a market one. Although the initial experiences in Hungary bode ill for women - women's jobs have been widely threatened by redundancies and closures, and vacancies for women have been decreasing - it is an over simplification to assume that the changes would have only a negative impact on the lives and economic activities of women. One fact needs special attention in this respect: unemployment figures do not show a significant difference between the sexes.

Women's jobs at risk

The first closures and cutbacks in male dominated heavy industries and similar changes made later in female-dominated light industries, which were due to the collapse of the Council for Mutual Economic Assistance (CMEA), both having an impact on women's employment. Major redundancies, partial closures and cuts in production in the steel and mining industries, where many women are employed in over-staffed administrative managerial departments, directly affect women's employment. Unemployment among the predominantly male mine and steel workers, whose wives have traditionally not worked as those industries are well-paid, could force those women to seek employment for economic reasons as it is highly unlikely that their husbands could again find such well-paid employment. Those women are being forced to enter the labour force at a time when vacancies for unskilled and semi-skilled workers are at their lowest and the competition strongest due to redundancies in various administrative areas.

Women workers who have been confined to low-paid, semi-skilled traditionally female jobs in textile, garment or manufacturing industries are also facing serious difficulties regarding the future of their jobs. Economic changes should result in a considerably streamlined and increasingly competitive market for Hungarian industries that exclusively or partially produces goods for the socialist market. It is not evident that companies whose trade is based in the socialist market would be able to adjust to the expectations of the western market. Loss of CMEA mar-

---

[*] by Maria Lado, Institute for Labour Research, Ministry of Labour.

kets will inevitably result in cutbacks and closures of some female-dominated industries and will certainly lead to increased unemployment among women.

To date no research has been undertaken on redundant women workers, nor are women accounted for in those few studies that focus on the redundancy process itself. That lack of attention is based on the assumption that redundancy or unemployment is less of a problem for women as they have a fall-back position of housewife. Whether women have been discriminated against in redundancy is difficult to determine. Larger redundancies suggest that men are more likely to be retained than women, but the reasons for that require further research. Redundancy, however, deserves special attention when analysing women's employment prospects, for at least three reasons. First, redundancy is one of the unavoidable adverse concomitants of economic restructuring, which might lead to serious social and political tensions. Secondly, it is the major source of recent unemployment. Thirdly, estimates concerning the scale of further redundancies are bleak.

One of the latest overviews, which gives special attention to women's employment prospects, argues as follows: "In 1991 there will be a further reduction of employees in nearly all spheres of production. According to the appraisal of the Research Institute of Economy, a 50-80 percentage drop in the Soviet export demand may result in the reduction of 120,000-130,000 employees in Hungarian industries if all indirect relevant effects are taken into consideration. Due to previous dismissals, the engineering industry intends to lay off more workers (11 per cent) than mining or metallurgy (9 per cent), light industry reckons with an 8 per cent reduction, while the food industry with 6 per cent. As the ratio of female workers is significant only in the two latter industries (66 and 44 per cent, respectively), the current male/female ratio among the unemployed is not expected to change considerably in industry. The same can be said concerning agriculture, where a reduction of 150,000-300,000 has been forecast, while women's participation rate in this branch of the economy is around 40 per cent. In the construction industry, domestic trade and transportation combined 40,000-50,000 dismissals are estimated. Among these branches, there is only one where women represent the majority of the workforce, and that is domestic trade. Another aspect of unemployment, which can hardly be estimated in numbers, is the increase of unemployment among intellectuals. The situation is expected to be critical primarily in public education. There will be drastic reductions of staff, and cultural institutions will be closed down if the current financial difficulties of local governments are not solved.

This will lead to growing female unemployment. As a counterbalance, increasing labour demand of banks, financial institutions and insurance companies provide employment possibilities for girls with secondary and high-level education".[1]

As all the above considerations are based on quite uncertain economic forecasts and are questionable as far as the methodology of their formulation is concerned, it cannot be concluded that women will lose their jobs to a greater or lesser extent than men. Whether women or men will be dismissed in greater number depends on many factors, such as the nature of the workforce reduction; extent of labour reserves in organization; occupational and age structure of trade unions and workers' mobility; and strategy and strength of trade unions and other worker groups. There are though certain factors that jeopardize women's chances when competing with men for keeping jobs. For example, family responsibilities, women's weaker representation in trade unions and their lagging behind men in vocational training. It also should not be forgotten that the services of women are usually regarded as being dispensable at a time of declining labour demand and, as such, women will inevitably face greater insecurity during the transition process.

Vacancies: for men only

Women experience the disadvantages of their gender more clearly in their search for a new job. Statistics on vacancies registered by the Employment Offices show that some 20-30 per cent of non-manual jobs and 65-70 per cent of manual jobs advertised exclude women. It is not clear that the reasons for the exclusion are fully objective ones. Job advertisements in the mass media more openly discriminate against women and the better the offered job the more likely that men only are encouraged to apply. That is particularly so for joint ventures and for senior managerial positions. Both women and the labour administration have been passive in their response to such discrimination and the broader consequences of women's exclusion from available jobs has not been discussed. Men's advantage over women in the job search could be explained by the persistence of traditional attitudes in that men are still regarded as the breadwinner and thus given priority in employment. More recently, employers' decisions on hiring have also been influenced by a tendency to make women withdraw from the labour market.

Back to household duties?

Historically women have been considered as a secondary workforce, a reserve army of workers,

[1] M. Frey, "Prospects of Women in the Transforming Hungarian Labour Market", delivered at the Tripartite Symposium on "Promotion Equality in Employment", organized by ILO (Prague, 14-18 October 1991).

whose function is to satisfy the ups and downs of the labour market need for workers. The post-war period saw many thousands of women entering the labour market to satisfy the need of industry for labour. Then, the economic reform of 1968, the aim of which was intensive development with more efficient use of resources, led to a sharp decrease in the demand for labour. It is not by chance that in 1967, child-care leave that offered leave to women until a child was three years of age was introduced in Hungary. That was a population policy measure officially intended to increase fertility but it is also quite clear that it also served to withdraw women from the labour market and thus decrease the possibility of unemployment. The combined threat of high unemployment and a decreasing population has become an argument for ousting women from the labour market. "There [was] no question that the expansion of employment among women resulted in a decline in fertility. But [was] it realistic to draw the conclusions that stopping the declining fertility trend would require limiting or even reducing female employment? ... The willingness of future female generations to have children cannot be increased successfully by limiting employment opportunities but by reducing the current employment tensions,"[2] and other burdens.

Another factor that limits women's economic activity or excludes them from the workforce is the provision of child-care facilities. Approximately 30 per cent of kindergartens are attached to the workplace and many of those have been closed down due to financial difficulties of the company. The other 70 per cent of kindergartens are run by the State and many have experienced difficulties associated with constraints operating on the State-budget. The question for women would no longer be how to combine paid employment with family chores but that of choosing between paid work and the family, and that would obviously be a major step back for equality of opportunity for women.

Unemployment among women

Interestingly, unemployment has affected women to a less extent than men in Hungary. Women were less represented than men among registered unemployed since the time data have been available on unemployment. In 1991 women's ratio among the unemployed varied between 37-42 per cent. Although women's ratio among the unemployed was lower than that of men among the economically active over the whole year, data show some warning tendencies. Women's rate among the unemployed rose steadily in 1991, while their participation rate in the economy declined considerably. The male/female ratio among

the unemployed was 61.2/38.8 in January 1991, and 58.3/41.7 in September 1991, while the same ratio concerning economic activity changed from 51.7/48.3 to 55.9/44.1 in the same period. Thus the unemployment rate increased faster among women (from 1.5 to 5.5 per cent) than men (from 2.2 to 6.6 per cent) over the same period.

What made the situation of the unemployed very hard was the reduction of vacancies. In December 1991 there were only 3 vacancies for 100 unemployed in comparison with 21 vacancies a year before. Thus, both sexes faced serious difficulties when looking for a new job and, as a consequence, there was no significant difference among them in the length of time they were unemployed.

In one respect, unemployment clearly caused more problems for women than men, and that was the level of financial provision. As unemployment benefits are calculated as a percentage of previous income, and women's income is usually lower than that of men, women's unemployment benefits could easily be too low to cover everyday needs. In 1991, 79 per cent of unemployed women got a benefit lower than the official minimum wage, while for men the figure was 55 per cent.

As to unemployment, the outlook is not promising. Estimates differ on its rate but agree that it will increase. Growing unemployment has its sources primarily in the deepening recession, in the strict anti-inflation policy of the Government and in the unavoidable difficulties of economic adjustment. Government sources estimate an unemployment rate of between 9 and 11 per cent for 1992, and forecast a slight decline for 1993 (8-10 per cent). How unemployment and its burdens will be shared between the sexes, and whether economic recovery will favour men or women, will depend on many factors. Special policies and measures are required, however, if women's equality is to be taken seriously, as women's special circumstances, such as family responsibilities and weak representation of their interests, could lead to an increase in women's vulnerability to future economic changes.

Special measures needed

Women are likely to face more difficulties than men adjusting to the new requirements and circumstances of the market economy because they have maintained their traditional roles in terms of domestic and child-rearing responsibilities. Due to that "double burden", married women, particularly those with children, have experienced great difficulties in im-

---

[2] K. Koncz, A gyermekvállalás társadalmi-gazdasági meghatározottságáról (On social-economic determinants of fertility), *Közgazdasági Szemle*, No. 11, 1987, p. 1350.

proving their knowledge or skills and are thus ill-prepared for the coming changes. Despite their high level of education, the majority of women lack professional skills that are a precondition for employment in the new jobs. Employers, moreover, tend to prefer "investment" in men who are considered more stable employees than women. The cost-benefit ratio of employing men is more favourable to employers. Lacking marketable, up-to-date skills with limited access to training, women's employment could easily become marginalized. Women's interests are also less well articulated and represented by the different trade unions than those of men. Neither the new trade unions nor the successors to the old "single" trade union have recognized the importance of women's issues. They have paid little or no attention to the special problems encountered by women. The women's movement is weak and women appear reluctant or not strong enough to make their voices heard.

Whether special assistance should be given to women to facilitate their adjustment to the market economy is a question that has not been given considerable attention before. The traditional gender-blindness in analysis of economic impact is largely responsible for that omission. That renders the nature of the assistance required difficult to determine but some basic rules could be formulated:

(a) Due to the controversial nature of established de jure equality and protective legislation, it appears better not to create too many new protective measures in the near future. The more protected women are the more isolated they are likely to become. Strong positive discrimination could harm women as much as negative discrimination. Attention should rather be given to the fulfilment and monitoring of existing legislation;

(b) Women should also become more active in seeking and establishing employment initiatives. As jobs become less available within the traditional framework of employment, more people would be pushed to create their own jobs. Women should be encouraged to break from traditional female occupations, to try something different;

(c) The measures aimed at easing the transition period should be diverse. Women cannot be regarded as a homogeneous group in terms of employment behaviour and attitudes towards work. Many variables, including age, educational background, work experience and market conditions influence the level of women's need for support over the transition period to a market economy. Flexible, varied measures, targeted on a particular stratum would be the most appropriate for the advancement of women throughout the transformation period.

B. Some aspects of the changing situation of women in the process of transition*

The collapse of the Communist regimes in east-central Europe have revealed significant differences in the situation of women in the countries concerned. Those initial diversities have been strengthened by the various economic and political developments in the region in the past two or three years. Such remarkable differences are surprising as it would be expected that the long-lasting uniformity of political structures, similarities of economy and existence of the same ruling ideology would have led to more standardization of basic social relations. That assumption has not been confirmed and many puzzling questions arise as to the differences in women's situation. Why has the democratization of political life led to the rapid emergence of quite powerful women's movements in some countries and not in others? Why did the transition period affect women more in some countries than in others? What were the social, economic and institutional factors behind the different rates of unemployment? Could those differences be accounted for by the different strategies

of privatization or were the answers rooted in sociological and historical factors? Similarly, could the move towards restricting access to abortion in some countries compared with its liberalization in others be explained merely by current political orientation or would different religious traditions and notions of family have to be examined? Many of those questions can only be answered by future research, but the aim of this paper is to contribute to the body of knowledge by an examination of trends and recent developments in Hungary.

The peculiar process of transition from a State-ruled to a market economy began before the political changes of 1989-1990. It would be more precise to say that the political changes were the outcome of the long-term erosion of the former State-socialist structure. And that erosion had gradually penetrated the foundations of institutions and relations in the spheres of production, distribution and consumption as well as in everyday life. Women played a major

---

*   by Julia Szalai.

part in that erosion. Although their contribution was not political in the classical sense, political consciousness was not lacking.

The vehicle of the gradual erosion has been the second economy. The daily participation in informal productive activities in addition to people's regular work in State-controlled firms has gradually become the norm. The vast informal sphere of production, that is, the second economy, is based on the cooperation and active participation of the (extended) family. Women share the workload but also manage the quite sophisticated organizational requirements of those small businesses. Their "secondary role" as wage-earners is used to determine the optimal combination of participation of all family members in the formal sector (dictated by legal, administrative and financial regulations) and in the informal economy (dictated by the aspirations and needs of the family). The ongoing work of optimizing and balancing often contradictory pursuits requires a number of planning, administrative and organizational skills that include the management of time, energy, relationships and material resources at the disposal of the family unit. Women have become expert at such skills. The success achieved by a substantial number of families could best be measured by the degree of affluence and standard of living of those families. The capacity of the second economy is enough to enable families to preserve previous standards amid the worsening conditions of the 1980s. The second economy has played a role in postponing and countervailing the unfavourable and serious impact of the crisis and general impoverishment and social disorganization.

The indispensable role women play in that process should be considered when analysing the recent trends of economic and social transformation. An adequate explanation for their participation as owners, co-owners or managers in the rapidly expanded private small enterprises, or on their relatively low rates among the unemployed, or even for the motivations behind their increased and well-targeted education activities can be given without taking into account the material and cultural aspects of their extensive experience in the second economy. Such participation has induced remarkable changes in their habits, orientations, aspirations, values and priorities. Although women's participation in the second economy also reinforces the traditional roles of men as the main earners and women as the main carers, the character, content and social meaning of those patterns has changed. The reproduction of the outwardly old models has been accompanied by an extensive and increasing participation of women in employment and other activities outside the family and the household. That combination gives women substantial independence and autonomy although within the framework of traditional relationships, but at the same time divorce is one result of the breakdown of the often fragile compromise between patriarchal relationships and career expectations. The break-down of marriages creates major problems for women. Single-parent families usually headed by women face exceptionally high risks of poverty, and the potential of the second economy to countervail economic hardship is limited for them.

The second economy is extremely important in determining the social status and material well-being of families. Data on educational attendance, regional occupational mobility, income and consumption patterns show that Hungarian society over the past 10-15 years has been increasingly divided into those who have been able to countervail the deepening economic crisis by intensification of their activities in the second economy and increased redistribution of resources within the family, and those who have no such back-up. Data on poverty show that urban families with several children are overrepresented in the latter group. The burden of poverty is carried by women. Although many women have a reasonable level of education (secondary or above), they are increasingly employed in unqualified jobs in industry or low-paid work in services and administration, where the threat of unemployment is high. The need for subsistence increases their defenselessness and has serious consequences for their everyday life, including childcare. While many favourable aspects of the long-term transition to a market economy can be observed, the negative features of increasing class-differentiation and the growing percentage of women in poverty should not be ignored. The diverging life-perspectives of women with similar education but different family background; the decreasing significance of merit and achievement as opposed to the increasing importance of heritage and informal support indicates potential serious conflicts and social disintegration that requires some form of social intervention. Attention should be drawn to the urgent need to formulate policies to ameliorate such conditions. The recent developments in the process of economic transition including modifications of childcare patterns and the concomitant growing inequalities introduced into women's lives because of childcare responsibilities are examined below.

An overview of the changing patterns of women's and men's employment

Full employment based on full-time work in State-regulated spheres of the economy characterized socialist societies and had particular consequences for women. The rapid extension of employment in the last decades was based on the "everlasting" growth of women's involvement in labour. The new industrial policy is based on access to semi-skilled and unskilled labour drawn from the masses of former agricultural workers and housewives who have never previously been in paid employment. Consequently, the employment rate of women aged 15-54 rose from 35 per cent in 1949 to 74 per cent in

1984. Women's semi-skilled and unskilled labour accounted for 27 per cent of the non-qualified labour force in 1949 and double that in 1984. The percentage of semi-skilled and unskilled blue-collar workers in the female labour force was 51 per cent in 1970 and only 44 per cent in 1980, while unqualified positions accounted for 46 per cent of all jobs in 1970 and 38 per cent in 1980. That trend continued in the 1980s. Despite their rising level of education, women are heavily overrepresented in the worst segments of the labour force.

The expansion of employment among women has been accompanied by a rise in their level of education. The percentage of women who have completed secondary education rose from 20 per cent in 1970 to 38 per cent in the mid 1980s. Women's education tends to be comprehensive rather than vocational, although the ratio of women who held qualifications for skilled work rose from 4 to 12 per cent between 1970 and 1984.

The result of this is the dominance of men in well-paid qualified jobs in all industries compared with women who are increasingly confined to lower paid, monotonous, blue- and white-collar jobs. Women's secondary status in the labour force is indicated by the significant differences between male and female monthly earnings. Despite differences in the amount of overtime worked and qualifications, the gap between earnings is largely attributed to sexual discrimination between men and women: better educated white-collar women tend to be in a relatively worse employment situation than their blue collar male colleagues.

The enforced participation of women in the labour market gave rise to feelings of guilt among many women because labour market activity was seen as incompatible with their roles as mothers and wives. Women thus desired more flexible working arrangements that allowed the satisfactory accomplishment of all their roles. Those feelings combined with economic considerations and the significant liberalization of economic and employment policy by the Communist Party led to the expansion of family-based small household-economies during the mid-1960s. Participation in and time devoted to the various activities of those self-productive small businesses has continuously risen since that time.

Although the most important fields of the second economy embraced first of all agricultural and constructional activities, people's participation in its more urbanized and more modernized sectors of services - repair work, catering, typing and childcare - has also increased.

Typical "female" and "male" jobs in the second economy follow traditional patterns of sexual division of labour but quite significant shifts have caused

men to take up traditional "female" tasks, especially in relation to children, and women to take up traditional "male" tasks, especially in construction and management. Most importantly, the content of "traditionalism" has changed and work for the family has become a source of pride and self-respect and the skills acquired in the informal sector are useful in the adaptation to a market economy. The second economy symbolizes autonomy, cooperation and success objectively and between men and women.

Women's extensive involvement in the household economy does not appear, as some critics argue, to constitute an increased conservatism of women, rather the opposite as recent changes in their labour-force participation rate suggests. Women's unemployment rate is lower in all age-groups than that of men. An explanation for that could be the greater adaptivity of women, in that they may be more likely to consider alternative forms of working and be less hampered by traditional concepts of their own role than men might. The rapid development of small private businesses might absorb a share of women's unemployment in, for example, part-time work. Women's former market experiences might also be used by such businesses though that form of employment is usually available only to the better educated and qualified.

A recent study found that 32 per cent of the owners/managers/members of the new small enterprises were women, most of whom had good schooling, and that women's participation rates exceeded the average in trading and small cooperatives. Market experience gained in other private/semi-private spheres of production is the most decisive and important element in choosing those forms of employment.

Women appear to have adapted well to the new economic circumstances but, as many changes are still underway, the long-term prognosis may not be so rosy. Women may become increasingly unemployed or forced into part-time work not of their choosing. Evaluation and continuous follow-up of those processes will be one of the most important tasks of social scientists in the near future.

Changes in the ways and patterns of childcare

The rapid expansion of the labour force in the socialist economy drew first of all on the generation of young women who were mothers and thus needed regular daycare for their children. The boom in public child-care facilities in the 1950s and early 1960s was in response to the rapid industrialization of Hungary. Children's needs were subordinated to political priorities and economic goals; quantity not quality became the goal as available capital was poured into industrialization rather than services. Thus child-care facilities were characterized as overcrowded, minimally supervised, physically inadequate, unhealthy and operating to rigid timetables, and incapable of providing personal and individual attention to children.

The serious inadequacies of the services became a matter of conflict in the late 1960s and 1970s when the quality of such care was not commensurate with improvements in living standards and family aspirations. A suitable solution was demanded, particularly by young families whose own private household provided much better conditions than did the child-care facilities. The result was probably the most significant innovation of the 1960s - the extension of choices for care of children aged up to three years by the introduction of the child-care grant in 1967.

In addition to the favourable impact on the lives of young families, and on the psychological and physical development of children, the grant was an important compromise between the political, economic and ideological principles of the regime and those of the people. The background to the Politburo decision to introduce a grant to encourage women to stay at home with their babies was complex. Reduced levels of production, the threat of unemployment that was meant to accompany the liberalization of economic management, the growth in the labour force as a result of the population policy of the 1950s, the scarcity of resources and increased demands for institutional childcare, all had an effect on the decision-making process. Public arguments in favour of helping mothers to stay at home for the first three years of a child's life were supported by pediatrics and, surprisingly, economists and planners. Studies on labour-force participation of women with young children showed that mothers of children up to two years spent 30-40 per cent of their total working hours either on sick-leave or unpaid leave due to the sickness of a child and, because such leave was unplanned, frequent disorders in production occurred. The ideal solution to both those problems, in addition to the problem of child health, appeared to be the child-care grant.

The grant was welcomed by diverse groups in society and its 20-year history has proved the early expectations. Overcrowding was eased in institutions providing childcare, women's health improved, particularly post-parturition, and children's health in all areas showed signs of improvement. Problems also arose, however, with the introduction of the child-care grant. It significantly contributed to a marked increase in social inequalities between families with children as the take-up rate of the grant was greatly influenced by professional and financial considerations. Lower educated, non-qualified women tended to take the grant much more often and for a longer period than their better-educated colleagues. Occupational promotion of young women also slowed as a result of the grant. Recently, however, the grant has lost much of its appeal even among less-qualified

women since its monthly value has not kept pace with rapidly increasing consumer prices. The take-up rate of the grant dropped in the first half of the 1980s, thus again straining the resources of nurseries. Women tended to return to work also because of the threat of unemployment. However, serious social and occupational tensions have accompanied those processes and urged the modification of the initial schemes. The introduction in 1985 of the earnings-related version of the former child-care grant helped to ease tensions and contributed to an increase in the birthrate in the late 1980s, though its consequences on the even more substantial increase of income differentials shifted the tension to other spheres.

Conclusions

The main tendencies of the period of the modification of socialism were the development of living conditions, modernization of the way of life and the gradual liberalization of the implementation of classical socialist rules. Hidden in those processes were two others: the steady increase of socially determined differentials and the widening of the gap between the public and private spheres of life. The form of the old system led to its erosion and economic crisis that manifested itself in decreasing economic performance, growing symptoms of social disintegration and increasingly dysfunctional important institutional networks, such as health care and social security. The consequences were a rapid increase in poverty, worsening health standards, growth of unemployment, high inflation and the general widening of social inequality between those who could and those who could not cope with the current difficulties and change.

Recent findings on the characteristics of those living in poverty show a marked shift towards an overrepresentation of young urban families with children. The decreasing real value of the child-care grant contributes to that situation: women at home on the grant are more than twice as numerous among the poorest as in the overall population. That form of poverty challenges the stated social policy of the past two decades: instead of promotion and preservation of public services and social security, haphazard emergency assistance is the focus. Interestingly, the risks of poverty are matched by the chance of affluence among families with young children. The increase in inequality among families with young children was more dramatic than for any other group of the population. The erosion of redistributive social policy and the emergence of markets forces, meant that poverty or affluence among families was exclusively determined by the capacities of the private sector. As those tendencies did not appear temporary or transitory they could have serious consequences for the long-term future of social cohesion and organization. Class-differences between women might turn to "cast-differences", locking the least supported poorest mothers into a cycle of neediness. Urgent social protection was required to prevent serious and

uncontrollable social conflicts that might shatter the fragile social integration.

IX. POLAND

A. Present situation of women*

Introduction

Women have traditionally held a special position in Polish society as models of patriotism and as people responsible for the life of the family, although the man was always considered the head of the family. Poland was one of the first countries in Europe to grant women the right to vote. Throughout the complicated history of the Polish nation, the struggle for freedom has always been an issue of major importance, and women have played an essential role in it, although not usually in leadership positions. Women participated in the underground movement during the Nazi occupation as well as in the Warsaw uprising in 1944. During the Second World War, more than 6 million people, a majority of them men, died. The burden of rebuilding at the conclusion of the War fell largely to women. Women became involved in many occupations and professions that were traditionally male, and started and managed a family. Under Communist rule women were encouraged to fulfil both their functions and often suffered public criticism if they performed only one function, whether that was productive or reproductive. Twenty years on, an alarmingly reduced birth rate combined with an artificial economic prosperity saw official propaganda encouraging women to return to the home to care for their families and to have at least three children. At the same time, and in violation of existing laws, there was a growing discrepancy between the salaries of men and women performing the same job. Communists encouraged women to join various Party structures that were supposed to demonstrate women's emancipation and lack of sexual discrimination. Yet those posts tended not to provide them with effective decision-making opportunities.

That situation is repeated in modern-day Poland. Women formed the basis of resistance against Communism and, as active members of the Solidarity movement, they organized help for those people persecuted after martial law was declared in December 1981. Women acted as the messengers in an underground opposition movement, and as editors and publishers in the clandestine press. Unfortunately, none of those activities had any effect on the outcome of the political and social position of women after the bloodless revolution and victory over the Communist régime in the spring of 1989. All the problems associated with the deep economic crisis in Poland and the difficulties of everyday life are mainly women's problems. Women bear the consequences of change in Poland. The transition from a centralized economy to a free market economy, and the accompanying unemployment, has created new problems and particular dangers for women.

The demographic situation of Poland

At the end of December 1990 Poland had a population of 38.2 million of which 21.2 million were women and 23.6 million lived in towns and cities. For every 105 women there were 100 men. After age 41 the proportion of women increased markedly, because of a very high mortality rate among men aged between 35-45. Over the age of 60, there were 145 women for every 100 men and at the uppermost age group, over 85 years of age, there were 190 women for every 100 men. There were significant demographic differences between urban and rural areas and between provinces depending upon the economic basis of the province and its proximity to a large city. There had been a gradual decrease in the number of women living in rural areas largely due to their migration to towns. In some rural provinces that meant that over half of the young men had no opportunity of finding a wife in the region in which they were living. In cities women outnumbered men by an average of 108 to 100. Women comprised 48.3 per cent of the working population but in urban areas there were 65 per cent of women of working age compared with 61.5 per cent of men. There had also been a dramatic and constant decrease in the birthrate. In 1990 the rate was 4.6 per thousand, the lowest since 1948. The low rate was attributable to a decrease in the number of live births, a relatively high number of deaths and constant emigration. The reproduction co-efficient was the lowest in Europe and the lowest in Poland since 1946. Bad health also played a part in that co-efficient, but so too did the situation of Polish women.

Women in politics: law, theory and practice

Harsh living conditions and everyday problems have led to the widespread conviction that sex discrimination has been legally sanctioned. Public knowledge of legislation is poor and that has led to numerous misunderstandings. A discrepancy exists between the law and its application. The Polish Constitution, written in 1952 and amended many times since, states in article 67, paragraph 2, that all citizens are equal "regardless of their sex", while

* by Zophia Kuratowska, Professor of Medicine and Vice-President of the Senate of Poland.

article 78, paragraph 1, confirms the equal rights of women and men in all fields of State, political, economic, social and cultural activities. All subsequent electoral laws have guaranteed active and passive voting rights for Polish citizens "regardless of their sex". Local government electoral law is similar. Equal rights for women, including in public activity, have also been granted and extended by the ratification of the Convention on the Elimination of All Forms of Discrimination against Women.

Women's right to participate in non-governmental organizations and associations that conduct political activity was also guaranteed by that Convention as well as a new law on associations of 7 April 1989. That law was worded in accordance with other international legal instruments on human and political rights. It guaranteed equal rights to all citizens to participate in their country's political life, to express their opinions and to realize their individual interest in various associations. Constitutional norms, outlined in such laws as the Employment Code, the Civil and Marital Code and the Insurance Law, form a comprehensive legal system that enables women to perform a full political and social role. In practice women's participation in decision-making is low. At the end of December 1990, women accounted for 12.7 per cent of State administrative staff at the rank of councillor or above and only 5.2 per cent of ministerial posts. In spite of legal guarantees of women's right to represent the State at an international level, the Ministry of Foreign Affairs is the institution with the lowest percentage of women holding managerial posts (0.5 per cent). No woman holds such a post in the Ministry of Defence or the Minitry of the Interior. There is only one woman ambassador and very few women holding diplomatic posts abroad. There are no women among the 49 local governors and when the new Government was formed at the beginning of 1991, the percentage of women employed in government administration significantly decreased.

The first fully democratic Senate and Sejm elections since the Second World War created an opportunity for women to begin a political career. It was anticipated that women would achieve appropriate representation. That did not happen. Of the 100 seats in the Senate women won only seven and in the Sejm they accounted for only 13 per cent of deputies. All women candidates from the Solidarity Civic Committee won parliamentary seats. The outcome of the elections was not due to sex discrimination but rather to the minimal involvement of the electorate in the process of selecting candidates and preparing lists of candidates. A similar situation occurred during the local elections in May 1990. Women accounted for 11 per cent of local government posts and that corresponded to the percentage of women who ran for those posts. This was a great surprise since it indicated that local problems were of concern to women and women had made the most valuable proposals for solving local problems during pre-election meetings.

Under Communist rule, women held 20 per cent of government posts. All posts were filled by a system of nomination, with candidates being chosen by the Party. Women who held government posts were largely without decision-making power. Thus an artificial situation was created and completely misinterpreted by women's movements in the West, for whom that situation was admirable and served as an ideal model. Women who currently hold public posts are much more active and the role they play is more important. Of six posts of deputy speaker in Parliament (three for each house), three are held by women. It seems no accident that those three women are medical doctors. That profession is characterized by a vast majority of women and, under Polish conditions, they require lots of energy, independence, responsibility and readiness to serve the public. Those features are advantageous in pursuing a political career.

Women's participation in political parties is difficult to estimate. In post-Communist Poland, the multi-party system is still in its infancy and parties are still not popular among a public that remembers the days of Communist Party domination. Except for two socio-democratic parties that emerged from the former Communist Party and in which women are quite active, and the remaining Communist satellite groups, there are no well-organized parties. Women's participation in peasant parties and extreme right groups is minimal. It seems that the Civic Movement - Democratic Action (ROAD) is the party in which women's participation is most significant and one that has a special women's section. In the leadership of eight of a parliamentary group formed by that party there are three women, and one of them is deputy chairperson. That, however, is an exception to the current parliamentary set-up. In view of the fact that women were active in Solidarity, it seems strange that in 1990 only four women were elected to sit on the National Solidarity Committee, which has 96 members.

Why have such good laws led to such poor results for women? Difficult living conditions including the lack of household facilities; time-consuming shopping procedures and irregular school-hours for children, particularly in the lower grades, have made it extremely difficult for mothers to plan their time. Women combine child and family care with professional employment, which has left them little time for hobbies and political activity. They therefore rarely ran for political posts. Women who do hold public posts are more rarely promoted than men even though their education is the same as their male colleagues. Furthermore, the traditional role division between women and men has left public activity to men, and home and family to women. That tradition has been strengthened by the Catholic model of the family, which places women in the home. The traditional upbringing in Poland has also resulted in a form of psychological resistance to women in managerial, political and professional posts. That resistance has deepened in the existing difficulties, assisted by unfavourable attitudes within society. Lastly, as the usual way of entering the political scene is via membership in a political party, and the existing parties and women's organizations are not strong enough, there are effectively no political forces that could prepare women to perform functions in government decision-making.

Women at work

Article 19 of the Polish Constitution reads: "Work is a right, a duty and a matter of honour for each citizen". Women have equal rights in all areas of activity, including work. The Employment Code guarantees women the right to receive the same salary as men, according to the principle of "the same salary for the same job". For many years women enjoyed complete equality of access to all forms of employment, including difficult work and night work. That situation has changed. A variety of rules, regulations and laws aimed at the protection of women's employment have been applied to working women in general or to specific groups of women, such as pregnant women and mothers of small children. Regulations govern the lifting and carrying of heavy objects, and 90 types of jobs in 18 branches of industry have been banned to women. Those are essentially underground work, work demanding great physical effort and work causing vibrations of the body, such as using a drill or driving a tractor (the symbol of emancipation during the 1950s). In practice, women often carry heavy boxes or sacks of products from storerooms to shop premises. Night shift, the legal duration of which should not exceed eight hours, is available to all women except those who are pregnant or have children under one year of age. Violations of that regulation occur either because the shift length is professionally impractical or because women want to work night shifts as they are better paid and they allow the daylight hours to be used for shopping and preparing meals, cleaning and taking care of children. Often women on a night shift have no time to rest.

More than 70 per cent of Polish women aged 18-60 work professionally and account for 45 per cent of the labour force. The majority of working women are aged 35-44. Women's share in State production industries is highest in several sectors including trade (69 per cent); communications (58 per cent) and industry (37 per cent). In manufacturing, women account for 37.4 per cent of the labour force with the highest percentage of women in the textile and electric industries. Women dominate in non-production areas with 70.1 per cent employed in that area. They account for 84.2 per cent of the labour force involved in finance and insurance, 80.2 per cent in health and social services, 76.3 per cent in education and 53.4 per cent in tourism and recreation. Women make up the majority of employees in primary schools, banks and post offices. In spite of the large proportion of women employed in government administration, Parliament and political parties, managerial posts are occupied by men. That situation also occurs in many industries whose workers are mainly women. However, due to privatization, women now often become owners and managers of shops, restaurants and drugstores.

The average wage of women is usually 30 per cent lower than that of men. In 1989 that difference was 21 per cent but it varied depending on the category of work and area of the economy in which employment was located. Women earn 30 per cent less than men in industry, 26 per cent less in tourism, 21-26 per cent less in transport and communications and 22.8 per cent less in health-care. Occupational differences also occur with female bookkeepers earning 66.3 per cent of male bookkeepers but bakers earning the same regardless of sex. The smallest gap of 2 per cent exists between male and female lawyers. The greatest discrepancy in wages occurs in the group aged 30-49 and the least in the group aged 50-59. Whether that gap constitutes discrimination is difficult to determine but statistically it appears to exist because women do not work in well-paid industries and do not hold supervisory posts. At the end of 1990, the Government established a uniform/equal/ basis for work evaluation that was applied to all State employees, regardless of their sex. Observance of those rules should result in the elimination of existing pay discrepancies between men and women holding the same posts. Women's professional financial promotion is delayed in comparison with men's. The delay is usually caused by child-rearing and family duties. The general retirement age for women is 60 and for men 65. Debate is ongoing as to whether the retirement age for women should be lowered to 55 or raised to 65. Standard of living, emotional and psychological well-being, financial status would all be affected by such a change. During a parliamentary debate on the new pension scheme in 1990, it was agreed that retirement age should not be lowered because the social security system would be over-burdened.

Unemployment came as a shock to a society based on full employment and people unused to searching for work not readily available. Hidden unemployment had existed for some time in the sense of over-employment. Factories and enterprises often employed many more people than they needed and that system of employment favoured uneconomical management and poor quality of work. It also led to the demoralization of the workforce and lack of initiative and enterprise. The new economic programme introduced in Poland at the beginning of 1990 could not have been implemented unless that situation was abandoned. In January 1990, there were 46,000 unemployed people in Poland and in December 1990 that figure had risen to 1,126,100, which constituted 8.3 per cent of the workforce. Women accounted for 51 per cent of that figure. Group redundancies in 1990, due to enterprise closures, affected 60 per cent of women. The majority of unemployed women were aged 31-40, which was of particular concern as that was a time of great financial expense for many involved in childcare. Unemployment was particularly difficult for women as there was a danger that they would become professionally and intellectually undervalued. Graduates of vocational high schools and of universities, particularly arts graduates, were in the most difficult situation. Often jobs existed, but in different regions, and migration to them was difficult due to lack of housing. Women were also discriminated against in candidate selection, because managers believed that women would have a higher absentee rate because of pregnancy and maternity leave. As a result women had to be more flexible in accepting employment outside of their profession including unskilled menial labour.

Prevention of unemployment particularly among women is one of the most important tasks of the State, trade unions and social organizations. Special training courses aimed at re-qualifying women and preparing them for professions in demand and special training for managerial posts should be undertaken. The women's section of Solidarity has been organizing such training with the assistance of French and American trade unions. Such initiatives, however, are limited and it is expected that the development of private enterprises will bring about a significant improvement in women's situation on the job market. Women would benefit from increased employment with flexible working hours and the possibilities of part-time work. The change in the economic system could favour that type of employment, and there are women achieving good financial and professional results as private business women who would be prepared to risk such enterprises.

Polish legislation provides a good system of protection for pregnant women including many regulations governing their employment. Pregnant women cannot be employed in strenuous jobs or jobs that might affect their health or the health of the child. Alternative employment must be provided to women in such a case and if the alternative is paid at a lower rate the enterprise is obliged to make up the difference. Pregnant women are banned from night shift and overtime but as women are not obliged to inform an employer of pregnancy, many women hide their pregnancy for as long as possible since not being employed on those shifts means a loss in wages. Women are entitled to fully paid maternity leave for a period of 16 weeks after giving birth to the first child and 18 weeks for any subsequent birth. Women cannot be dismissed during pregnancy or maternity leave and are guaranteed a return to the same job on completion of the maternity leave. Upon completion of maternity leave a woman can take educational leave for up to three years to care for the child without severing her employment connection. The period of educational leave, however, causes significant financial loss and is impossible to recoup and often creates a professional gap difficult to bridge that results in reduced earnings upon return to work. The existence of the benefit also discourages employers from hiring women. Men are given the possibility of taking educational leave but psychological barriers and traditional perceptions of men and women's roles limit the number who do so, although their number is growing. In addition to maternal and educational leave, women are entitled to short-term leave in the case of illness of a child or other duties connected with their rearing. The current legislation, thus, appears modern and sufficient as too much legislation or relief would ultimately worsen women's situation on the job market.

Women in rural areas

Approximately 27 per cent of women lived in rural areas and worked on private farms. Many work at other jobs at the same time. The working life of a rural woman is between 15 and 80 years, regardless of pension rights. As many as 65 per cent of women aged over 65 are active in farming, whereas in other professions only 2 per cent of women work until that age. There is no question of educational leave. Rural families maintain the tradition of large families. In 1988 the average number of children in city families was 1.74; it was 2.1 in rural families. Village women work extremely hard under often difficult conditions with limited modern conveniences, including running water and village shops. Young girls often migrate to the city seeking husbands and an easier life. That combined with the longer life-span of women results in approximately 30 per cent of farms being run by women, often elderly. In spite of the hard work, many more women express satisfaction with working on a farm than working in industry. In addition, strong family ties and traditions exist in the villages, expressed in three times fewer divorces than in the cities.

Women at school and university

Women are guaranteed by law equal access to all levels of education. In the school year 1989/90, 57.8 per cent of girls who finished elementary education continued at high school and technical and vocational schools. Girls accounted for 58.7 per cent of the total number of students in various types of high school and as much as 75 per cent at high school, including adult evening classes. Girls tend to predominate in schools that prepare students for traditionally feminine fields of further and higher education and professions. In 1988, for example, women constituted 85.9 per cent of students in medical service schools and 59.3 per cent in fine art schools but only 25 per cent in technical schools. Moreover, in general high schools girls account for 82.5 per cent of students enrolled in the humanities, 78 per cent in the arts, 76.3 per cent in the natural sciences and 53.5 per cent in the applied sciences. The scientific and technical curricula offered at high schools overrepresented by women is often inadequate, and it ill-prepares women for employment and limits their access to higher education. Women account for 51.6 per cent of students enrolled in higher education courses. Over 40 per cent of agricultural higher school graduates are women and almost 50 per cent of graduates of law and administration departments are women whereas only 17.9 per cent of graduates from higher technical schools are women.

Women who held a university degree make up 4.9 per cent of the total female population in Poland compared with 6.4 per cent for men. A low rate for both men and women. The careers of female graduates vary according to their family situation. In 1989 only 17.7 per cent of them held managerial posts and the largest group of them were found in the education system. Women account for over 73 per cent of elementary and school directors. The situation at universities is quite different. Very few women are rectors or deputy rectors and women account for 21 per cent of university professors, mainly in the humanities and medicine departments. Women usually take longer to complete higher scientific degrees and degrees of medicine and technology. Family duties and traditional attitudes of employers are largely responsible.

Women's health

The economic situation, a highly polluted environment, inefficiency of the health system, lack of preventive medicine, smoking, alcoholism, poor diet and lack of physical exercise and rest all contribute to the general poor health of the population. Women's health is particularly poor. The average life expectancy is 71 years, 75 years for women. The major health problem and principle reason for death is heart and circulatory disease. Poland has the second highest rate of death from heart disease in Europe. The number of women's deaths due to heart disease has risen rapidly. Approximately 12 per cent of women suffer from coronary disease. Women also suffer more often than men from strokes. In 1988 the death rate of Polish women due to heart attacks and strokes was 59 per cent higher than among the female population of other European countries. High blood pressure, diabetes and excessive weight are common ailments. Approximately 35 per cent of women over 45 years of age and 10 per cent of women aged

between 30 and 45 suffer from advanced spine and joint degeneration and osteoporosis. Working conditions often contribute to those diseases. Lung cancer has increased particularly among women, of whom over 50 per cent over 17 years of age smoke. Poland has a high death rate due to breast and uterine cancers as those diseases are usually detected too late for treatment. Lack of information and adequate screening techniques contribute to that situation. Pregnancy and birth bring their own health problems. Over 60 per cent of pregnant women suffer from anaemia and the death rate among pregnant women is high: 22 of 100,000 births result in the mother's death. In 1989, 8.5 per cent of newborn babies in Poland weighed less than 2.5 kilograms and the death rate among newborn babies was 18 per thousand.

Abortion

It is estimated that approximately 600,000 abortions are performed each year in Poland. Quite often a woman has several abortions within a year. The age at which girls have an abortion is becoming younger because of earlier sexual involvement. Abortion is used as a method of contraception as contraceptives are neither advertised nor readily available. Sex education is sketchy. Abortions are related to social and economic problems. Low income, inadequate housing, a partner's alcoholism or even fear of public disapproval, although that factor has decreased in importance in urban areas, are all reasons for women seeking abortions. Fear of losing their job is another reason women give for abortion.

The problem of abortion is complex, particularly in Poland with its strong Catholic influence. The 1956 law on abortion, in force until recently, was very liberal. In 1990, a draft law on the protection of the foetus, based on Church teachings, was approved by the Senate. The draft law allowed for abortion in cases of rape and a threat to the woman's life and provided penalties against doctors who performed abortions. That law became the focus of political struggle and caused sharp social conflict. The draft law is currently being discussed by the Sejm and if passed would have significant consequences for society and for women in particular, including an increased birth rate, the development of an underground abortion system, increased number of unwanted children and limiting women's right to choose. Before passing such a law, adequate steps should be taken to prepare society and public institutions for the new situation.

Single mothers

Should abortion be made illegal, there would be an increase in the number of women bringing children up alone. Various public and church groups have initiated activities to assist girls who give birth without the assistance of families and friends. Special homes have been established for that purpose. They are short-term measures only. Shortages of housing and unemployment are further obstacles to normal family life for those women. Single mothers constitute 13.7 per cent of the total number of Polish families and that percentage has grown during the last decade. Widows make up 60 per cent of single mothers, divorced women account for 10 per cent, unmarried women for 8 per cent and women permanently or temporarily abandoned by their husbands the remaining 20 per cent. The financial situation of single mothers is very difficult as they often live below the poverty line. Over 60 per cent of single mothers feel insecure as far as their basic living conditions are concerned.

Elderly women

Women constitute the majority of elderly people in Poland. Women account for 53.5 per cent of all handicapped people regardless of age, but the number of handicapped women over 60 is quite high. Elderly women suffer from a variety of disorders associated with age that are more common among city dwellers. Care for the elderly is generally insufficient and does not promote their independence. Many obstacles exist to their mobility.

Prospects and limitations

A significant gap exists between the Polish legal system and the reality of everyday life for Polish women. Legal regulations guarantee equal rights for women and men, legal protection is afforded to women in a variety of situations, including pregnancy, and discriminatory provisions are not in evidence. The law is not confirmed in practice, particularly in participation in political life, employment, earnings and family duties. Discriminatory practices against women arise largely from the difficult economic situation combined with adherence to traditional social models that includes public roles for men and household functions for women.

Women's situation will become even more difficult in the coming years regardless of the legal system. Women will become the main victims in the transition from a centrally planned economy to a free market, particularly in the sphere of employment. Dramatic limitations in the public infrastructure, including the provision of nursery schools, would also adversely affect women and their participation in social life. The traditional model of women is also resurfacing and being reinforced by the Catholic Church, Christian, nationalist and rightist groups. Such groups will probably gain more support and influence in the near future. Greater discrimination against women is to be expected in terms of "women's noble vocation".

If such consequences for women are to be avoided it will be necessary to establish and maintain modern and consistent social policies. Thus it will also be necessary to establish a women's lobby. An office intended to deal with women's problems was established within the Ministry of Labour but is currently being reorganized. However, a parliamentary group could be organized to deal with women's issues in the broadest sense. Non-governmental social organizations and foundations could be formed in affiliation with new political parties and women's newspapers. One of the most important tasks is to overcome the difficulties women have in running the household. Changes in production schedules and the creation of a network of institutions to provide assistance to families could both help. Changes should also be made in the education system and traditional stereotypes abolished, while joint responsibility for family and the equality of the sexes should be promoted.

People in Poland are becoming aware that it is not possible to create a truly democratic State without women's full and active participation. And that their participation is not possible if they are not able to exercise their legal right to freely choose a career and to engage equally with men in political, professional and family activities. The reform period could provide such an opportunity for Polish women.

B. The role of national machinery for the advancement of women in the changing political and economic situation*

The fourth anniversary of the creation of national machinery for the advancement of women was celebrated in Poland on 1 September 1990. The office of the Government Plenipotentiary for Women's Affairs was established in 1986 by the Council of Ministers as the first and only national machinery in central and eastern Europe. The Plenipotentiary was entrusted with the task of coordinating activities aimed at ensuring women's equal rights in all spheres of State, political, economic, social and cultural life as well as of improving the conditions of women's lives.

_____

*   by Grazyna Budziszewska, Office for Women's Affairs, Ministry of Labour and Social Policy.

In addition to the appointment of the Plenipotentiary, the Council of Ministers also adopted a programme of activities for the advancement of women that consisted of 22 areas of action to be implemented in the period 1987-1990. Central and local organs of State administration were made responsible for the implementation of that programme while the Plenipotentiary performed a coordinating role and prepared reports for the Government. At the same time, the Plenipotentiary was entrusted with the task of coordinating international cooperation in the field of women's issues and particularly to supervise the implementation of the Convention on the Elimination of All Forms of Discrimination against Women and to prepare reports to be submitted to the Committee on the Elimination of Discrimination against Women and to disseminate in Poland international standards regarding women's issues.

The changing political and economic situation in Poland has brought about both positive and negative changes in the situation of the population. Among the positive changes are increased opportunities for participation in the life of the country and an improved supply of consumer goods, while the negative effects are unemployment and hardship connected with the stabilization process. Women are much more affected by the negative effects than men on account of their greater family and home responsibilities, weaker labour market position and political involvement. In such a changed environment, the role of the Plenipotentiary for Women's Affairs should also change. How that organization has responded to the changes and the directions it may take in the future are discussed below.

Equal rights for women

Women are not discriminated against in the Polish legal system according to the precepts of article 1 of the Convention. Polish legislation contains provisions that refer equally to men and women. Where different provisions are made for women, they are protective ones that account for women's psycho-physical features and biological functions. The fundamental transformations undertaken in Poland require adjustment not only of basic economic laws but also of those regarding social policy and employment. One of the basic goals of the Plenipotentiary for Women's Affairs is to ensure that women's rights are safeguarded during that process.

One difficulty associated with that task is ignorance of the details of existing legislation, especially among women's organizations. Consequently, women are often not in a position to benefit from their legal rights nor to effectively fight for their full and universal implementation. The law is often contradicted by the practice and the situation has deteriorated with the expansion of private enterprises as private employers often feel that only socialized enterprises are bound by the labour law. As women might easily become the victims of that process there is an urgent need to eradicate women's legal illiteracy. The Plenipotentiary for Women's Affairs is concerned with the situation and that should give rise to the development of a comprehensive programme of action to improve the situation. The full commitment of the Government and cooperation from non-governmental organizations and the mass media are essential for the success of the programme.

Employment

Growing unemployment and competition on the labour market affects women to a greater degree than men. At the end of February 1991 the number of registered unemployed persons in Poland was 1,264,000 or 10 per cent of the labour force. Women accounted for 51 per cent of the total unemployed, the majority of whom were aged 31-40 years although the unemployment rate for young women was even higher than for young men. At the end of February 1991, there were 29.8 unemployed persons per vacancy, or 20.4 men and 53.5 women. The existence of so few vacancies for women arose for a number of reasons: for health reasons women are not permitted to perform the range of jobs that men can; particular occupations are traditionally performed by men and women lack the necessary vocational skills to undertake those jobs; women were more likely to have skills appropriate for administrative work, which was the first area to be affected by reductions in employment; and women's availability for work was lower than men's and their absenteeism was higher owing to their home and family responsibilities due to adherence to traditional division of roles and responsibilities between men and women. It should be noted, however, that women's employment is protected in the event of maternity and child-care leave.

Studies undertaken by the Ministry of Labour and Social Policy indicate that at the beginning of 1990 unemployment among men had increased more than among women but that that situation had stabilized and could reverse as a result of changes taking place in industrial areas that largely employ women. For those reasons, many more women than men need some form of retraining particularly in those areas where there is a high ratio of unemployed women to vacancies. Unfortunately, existing programmes for vocational training of the unemployed do not take into account the particular needs of women. It should be the aim of central and local administrative organs to change that situation. The Plenipotentiary for Women's Affairs should have an important role to play both in promoting such retraining programmes for women and in providing assistance to women to help solve other employment problems.

Female participation in decision-making

Polish legislation ensures women equal rights to participate in the formulation of government policy and in the implementation of policy as well as to hold public office and to perform all public functions at all levels of government. In practice, however, women's participation in decision-making is disproportionate to the level of their education and employment. Although women represent 28.1 per cent of managerial staff (a category ranging from foremen to key posts in the State administration), their advancement usually stops at lower and medium levels. The higher the management level, the lower women's representation.

In 1990, the Plenipotentiary for Women's Affairs carried out a study on women's representation among managerial staff in State administration. The results indicate that women represent only 12.7 per cent of that staff and that at the post of minister only 5.2 per cent, although the majority of persons employed in the civil service are women. The highest rate of female participation in managerial staff is in the Ministry of Culture and Arts, the Ministry of Health and Social Protection, and the Ministry of Labour and Social Policy. The lowest rate is in the Ministry of Foreign Affairs, the Ministry of International Economic Co-operation, the Central Planning Office and the Ministry of Justice. Even in ministries that have a high proportion of women among managerial staff, only a few of those women exceed the level of deputy director of a department. There are no women ministers, either, in the present cabinet.

Women's low level of participation in decision-making posts largely results from the traditional division of responsibilities between men and women. Women devoted much more time than men to the home and rearing children. The effect of the division of roles is carried over into the workplace and maintained in the social consciousness.

Few, if any, women are represented in the upper echelons and executive bodies of political parties, trade unions or associations. Women's organizations appear too weak to effectively prepare women for political functions. That situation was manifested in the recent elections for the Sejm and Senate in the Parliament where women acquired, respectively, only 13 and 6 per cent of mandates. Similarly, in local government elections 11 per cent elected were women, but only 6.4 per cent of the managerial positions in local administration are held by women. Both in the Parliament and local government, however, women are very active initiating legal acts and competing for the chair of deputies' clubs. The overall unsatisfactory level of women's political participation requires a long-term commitment from social and political women's organizations and groups and the mass media in addition to the Plenipotentiary for Women's Affairs to educate women and promote their participation in political and social life.

Cooperation with women's organizations and groups

Recently only three large women's organizations operated in Poland: the League of Polish Women, the Organization of Circles of Rural Housewives and the National Committee of Women in Cooperatives. They ceased operating in the new socio-economic situation. New grass-roots women's organizations, however, began to emerge. A number of them have functioned informally since the mid-1980s and they have already acquired the status of associations or have applied for registration. Membership of feminist movements varies but usually does not exceed 200 persons, the majority of them intellectuals and based in urban areas. Their agenda is to protect of women's rights, to eliminate all forms of discrimination against women, to combat anti-abortion laws and to ensure great accessibility to modern contraceptives for women. In addition to those groups, women's sections have emerged in trade unions and political parties. Their aim is the prevention of unemployment among women and the equal treatment of women within employment.

The role of women's organizations and groups might and should be critical in promoting women's activity, preparing women for decision-making positions and assisting women in difficult economic situations. The Plenipotentiary for Women's Affairs is cooperating with the majority of non-governmental women's organizations and groups and with female press and research workers dealing with women's problems. In addition, a permanent forum for cooperation and discussion has been established and called the "Women's Forum". All questions and problems connected with the social, political and economic advancement of women and their equality are debated and information is provided on activities for women carried out at the international level, mainly by the United Nations. Unfortunately, the meetings of the Forum have been disrupted because of the change of Government and a temporary vacancy in the post of the Plenipotentiary for Women's Affairs.

International cooperation

The important role played by international cooperation should be emphasized. Such cooperation has allowed Poland to benefit from the experience of other countries in dealing with similar problems associated with the advancement of women. In particular the cooperation of the United Nations is appreciated. The last session of the Commission on the Status of Women and the present Seminar were organized in the framework of preparations for the Fourth World Conference on Women to be held in 1995 that would be connected with a general appraisal of the application of the Nairobi Forward-looking Strategies for the Advancement of Women. The role that could be played by regional cooperation in Europe is also very important. Again the present Seminar is an example of such cooperation. The East-West Conference of Women's Issues within the framework of the activities of the Council of Europe, which will be held at Poznan, Poland, in December 1991, will also be important. The general theme of that Conference will be the effects of the political, economic and social changes in Europe on the situation of women.

The increased responsibilities of the Polish na-

tional machinery for the advancement of women have resulted in a change in its placement and its structure. The intention of Prime Minister Bielecki was to upgrade that machinery and on 2 April 1991 the Council of Ministers adopted a resolution on the Government Plenipotentiary for Women and Family, to be situated in the Cabinet of the Prime Minister, and gave to the Plenipotentiary much greater rights and possibilities compared with those entrusted to the Government Plenipotentiary for Women's Affairs that was situated in the Ministry of Labour and Social Policy. On 5 April 1991 Prime Minister Bielecki nominated Mrs. Anna Popowicz for the post of Government Plenipotentiary for Women and Family.

C. The impact of restructuring in political and economic spheres on the status of women*

Legal equality

Polish women gained legal equality in the Constitution of 1952. No further legislative or other means have been taken to ensure the practical implementation of that principle. Article 2 of the Discrimination Convention has, thus, never been implemented. The anti-discrimination paragraph of the Polish Criminal Code does not include discrimination with regard to sex.

Although the Polish People's Republic (1945-1989) was a country with a history of violations of human rights and basic freedoms, the period of restructuring has highlighted such discrimination. One of the rights granted to women was in the abortion bill of 1956. Very restrictive at first, the bill was later liberalized in its interpretation to allow abortion almost on demand.

Economic reforms and women's participation

The general perception in Poland has always been that the economy is based on production that is based on workers thus unpaid family workers, mainly women, have not been granted recognition in that process. Women's activity outside of productive activity has been traditionally taken for granted or ignored as a form of economic contribution. Conversely, women's reproductive role has been seen as in conflict with their productive role. The Polish Labour Code thus granted women equal right to work but because of their reproductive role banned them from performing certain jobs. That list included 90 jobs in 18 fields of production with an unhealthy or

dangerous environment or requiring physical strength. Women were, thus, not allowed to work as tractor or bus drivers. That list coincided with the list of men's top-earning jobs. No attempts were made to implement ILO Convention No. 89 on night work with regard to women but after the 1989 elections, the Solidarity Trade Union attempted to implement that Convention in the Warsaw Steel Works. It failed due to the organized resistance of women.

The Polish Labour Code also includes a series of protective regulations governing pregnancy and women with children. Pregnant women are not allowed to work at jobs dangerous to their health, nor are they allowed to work overtime or on night shifts. Women have the right to refuse to travel as representatives of their firms. Mothers were entitled to maternity leave of 16 to 18 weeks, fully paid. Fathers were only entitled to take that leave if the mother was dead. That has recently been changed and both parents can take leave for up to two years, paid at 25 per cent of the average monthly wage. Mothers are also entitled to fully paid leave in the case of illness of the child. A father's right to that leave was revoked in 1975, and fathers can only take a similar leave if both the mother and the child are sick. Pregnant women and women on maternity leave are protected against dismissal except if they violate their duties as a worker or if their place of employment closes down. In 1990 one extra condition was introduced. Pregnant women and women on maternity leave could be dismissed as part of a group of women dismissed as a result of restructuring, as part of what were termed "group reductions".

---

* by Jolanta Plakwicz, The Polish Feminist Association.

Women constituted 45.7 per cent of the workforce in 1989. Of 8 million working women, 5.5 million worked in the public sector and of those, 59 per cent worked in production. Almost half of that 59 per cent worked in industry and 26 per cent in trade. The most feminized areas of employment are trade, communications and industry, especially light industry. Women account for 69.7 per cent of trade workers and 58.7 per cent of communication workers. Women also account for 84.5 per cent of workers in finance and insurance, 80.5 per cent of health-care and social-welfare workers, 76.5 per cent of workers in education and 61.0 per cent of workers in culture and art. Educated women are mainly teachers, economists, physicians, lawyers, chemists, dentists, and building and chemical engineers.

Women accounted for 51 per cent of the unemployed in 1990 and of those 15.5 per cent were fired due to group reductions. There was 1 vacancy for every 37 unemployed women compared with 1 for every 10 unemployed men. No training or retraining schemes exist for women. The general tendency is to guarantee men's employment to ensure they can maintain their families. The fact that women work from economic necessity particularly those women who head single-parent families that account for 13.7 per cent of families is ignored.

Rural women constitute 27.2 per cent of all women in Poland and 75.1 per cent of them are economically active. Polish agriculture is facing severe difficulties but no government programmes have been initiated to contend with those. Women's wages were 21 per cent less than men's wages in 1989. The gap is larger in blue-collar occupations than in white-collar occupations. The disproportion is nowhere less than 10 per cent except in the two top-paying occupations of lawyer and mathematician, where the disparity is less than 3 per cent.

Participation in the decision-making processes

As a result of the May 1990 elections, women account for 25.5 per cent of local self-government body members. Young women aged under 30 years were mainly elected in rural areas but none were elected as a member of Warsaw local governments. No woman was appointed in the Government under Prime Minister Jan Olszewski (1991). In the Polish Parliament of 460 members in 1991, 42 were women and 7 out of 100 senators were women. The percentage of women represented in leading government posts is low and decreasing. In terms of the director and vice-director level, of 40 persons of that rank in the Office of the Council of Ministers, 3 were women; of 28 persons of that rank in the Ministry of Labour, 9 were women; of the 27 in the Ministry of Industry, 1 was a woman, and of the 30 in the Main Statistical Office, 12 were women. There are no women leaders of a political party and no women heads of Solidarity Trade Unions divisions. There is no woman in the President's Office any more, and only one woman ambassador.

Policy changes relating to the role of women and men in society

In the majority of Polish households domestic work is done by women and the division of domestic duties has shown no change since 1983. Sharing of family responsibilities generally means sharing decisions about the family budget and child-rearing, and planning family activities rather than domestic chores. Women tend to be assisted in their domestic chores by their mother or mother-in-law rather than by their husband. Despite equal rights to property and equal status in the family accorded to Polish women in the civil law code (1965), women do most of the domestic work and are the main carers of the young, the sick and the elderly.

A powerful trend has developed in Poland, supported by the Catholic Church, to eliminate the majority of family-planning options. The abortion bill of 1956 was severely restricted by the Government in April 1990 to be replaced with a Senate bill on the protection of the unborn. The Senate's bill (pending in the lower chamber) would forbid abortion in all cases except where there was a direct threat to life and in cases of legally proven rape. In 1991, the doctors corporation approved of a new ethical code that forbids doctors to perform abortions for indications other than a direct threat to life, health or in case of rape. The code is an open violation of the 1956 abortion act. Sexuality and family-planning issues have been excluded from education programmes in schools and the availability of contraception, scarce as it is, is seriously threatened by both the pending abortion bill and pro-life attacks against pharmacists selling contraceptives.

The Charter of Family Rights, the Catholic Church document determining women's social role, is a base for Solidarity trade-union work on a family wage programme as a means of pulling women off the labour market.

National machinery

At the level of the Polish Government, since 1991 women's issues are dealt with by the Government Plenipotentiary for Women Affairs and Family. The Plenipotentiary is not a member of the Council of Ministers, has no executive power and no financial means. Since 1978, Poland has had an ombudsman (civil rights spokesperson). In her four-year tenure she managed to win only in 23 per cent of cases. In 1990, a women's parliamentary club was established. A number of women's organizations have created a network for women's issues and family planning.

X. ROMANIA

A. Present situation and trends affecting women*

The revolution of December 1989, which removed the totalitarian regime, brought many political, economic and social changes to Romania. Those changes were to form the foundation of a new Romanian society built on the principles of democracy, freedom and human dignity; political pluralism and the separation of legislative, executive and judicial powers; and the guarantee of those principles in law. The revolution was followed by a period of preparation for parliamentary and presidential elections, which took place on 20 May 1990.

The Parliament is composed of the Assembly of Deputies and the Senate, both of which combined in a common sitting to form the Constituent Assembly for the adoption of the Constitution. Until such time as the Constitution is adopted the Parliament is to act as the legislative assembly. Within two years of the adoption of the Constitution further elections are to be organized by the Parliament. The President of Romania, who cannot be a member of a political party or organization, has the power to promulgate laws and to nominate the Prime Minister from among the representatives of the majority party in Parliament. The Government, as the central body of executive power, undertakes the public administration of the country. The composition of the Government is suggested by the Prime Minister and approved by the Assembly of Deputies and the Senate.

Women are not well represented in those top decision-making bodies. The Government has 23 ministers, all of whom are male, and 59 State Secretaries all but 1 of whom are male. Of the 397 Deputies in Parliament, 22 are women, and of the 119 Senators, only 1 is a woman. The President is a man. The composition of other senior decision-making bodies reflect the situation in Parliament. The Romanian Group of Inter-Parliamentary Union has 25 members of whom 1 is a woman; the Parliamentary Group of Friendship Romania-France has 71 members, 4 are women; and the Committee for the Support of Institutions for Child Protection has 24 members, of whom only 4 are women.

Human rights and legal equality

During the short period since the revolution, a series of measures have been introduced to guarantee European and universal standards of human rights and fundamental freedoms. At the legislative level, the first act adopted was designed to repeal existing laws, decrees and regulations enacted by the previous regime that were contrary to the interests of the Romanian people. Additional acts, asserting and observing fundamental rights and freedoms, include abolishment of the death penalty and authorization of public meetings. A number of new regulations governing labour practices have been enacted although a new Labour Code has not yet been adopted. As priority is given to areas that have direct and immediate consequences for Romanian life, a new Constitution has not yet been drafted.

The legal status of women was also reconsidered after the revolution. This was undertaken within the general context of fundamental human rights and freedoms but also involved drafting new regulations, particularly relating to family planning. A number of other measures were adopted that, although general in nature, have positively affected the status of women. A five-day working week was introduced, inequities in wages were removed, wage increases and promotions were granted and freedom to leave and to return to the country was granted. It should be emphasized that the legislation which existed prior to the revolution did not as a rule discriminate against women, however, de jure equality was not reflected in de facto equality. The role and significance of existing legal regulations and where appropriate amendments to those as they affect women are discussed in that light.

The 1965 Constitution specified that a Romanian citizen, without distinction to national origin, sex, race or religion had equal rights in all spheres of economic, political, legal, social and cultural activity and that no restrictions of those rights and no obstruction in their exercise was allowed on those bases. The old electoral law that accorded all Romanian citizens who reached the age of 18 years the right to vote has been amended to include, most importantly, without distinction to sex or political conviction. The newly introduced rights to associate that incorporate the right to organize and to organize public assemblies do not discriminate on the basis of sex. Article 23 of the Constitution also incorporates the principle of equality between women and men and provides State protection of marriage and the family and the interests of the mother and child. Romania ratified the Convention on the Elimination of All Forms of Discrimination against Women by decree in 1981.

The right to education, recognized in article 10 of the Constitution, was developed in the law on edu-

---

*   by Dimitra Popescu, Professor of Law.

cation and instruction. Article 2 of that law provides the right to education without distinction of nationality, race, sex or religion and without any restriction that could constitute discrimination. In the past this instruction had been violated on political, religious and social grounds among others. As a result of legislative measures and the creation of appropriate material conditions the university year 1990/91 was a landmark in free access to education. During this period a large number of private higher education institutes were established and an increased number of places were made available in existing State institutes.

Existing labour legislation also enshrined the principle of the right to work and equal pay for equal work without reference to discrimination between men and women. However, as there were a number of anomalies in that legislation it has been amended to ensure that the freedom to work is guaranteed without limitation to all citizens without distinction and according to their aspirations. Other provisions of the Labour Code and related regulations ensure that opportunity for employment is not limited by sex, that equal pay is guaranteed for equal work, that choice of occupation and function is not limited by sex and that employment conditions are favourable to the maternal function of women. Some of the regulations, such as those concerning the private sector however, adopted at the same time as measures were implemented to facilitate the transition to a market economy, do not contain firm principles of equality of men and women. Although the law on commercial companies, for example, does not contain restrictions relating to sex neither does it specify that distinctions are not to be made on this basis. Of most concern, however, is the regulation governing the hiring of staff, which allows for wages to be established by free agreement between the parties concerned although minimum wage limits must be observed. In essence the article is just but in practice women, particularly those with young or several children, may be disadvantaged by such free agreements. Women may be similarly disadvantaged by the regulation governing the engagement of wage earners depending upon proficiency, by which the organization employing the worker sets the conditions of engagement.

In view of those difficulties with the legislation, additional measures were needed to ensure adequate protection of women. To this end in order to ensure that women were not discriminated against at marriage or during maternity, article 146 of the Labour Code prohibits the termination of a labour contract in the event of pregnancy, during maternity leave, during periods of leave taken to care for a sick child and during the period when a woman's husband is doing military service. Conditions governing maternity were also improved immediately following the revolution. Women were granted paid leave at the rate of 65 per cent of the monthly wage to care for children up to one year of age in addition to the 112 days allowed for pregnancy and confinement. Income and pension rights were also guaranteed to employed women in case of sickness of a child up to three years of age. Additional benefits payable included grants to mothers with many children, grants for the birth of a child and monthly child support, the amount of which depends on the number of children but differences between urban and rural areas have been removed.

Social security regulations were also improved. Women had the right to receive a pension upon retirement from work with the age of retirement set at 55 years (60 for men), or 50 years (55 for men) if seniority exceeded the legal minimum of 25 years (30 years). For the calculation of seniority, the period during which a woman was entitled to work reduced hours to care for children under six years of age, was considered as full-time employment. In the calculation of years of uninterrupted service, interruptions made by a woman to care for a child up to seven years of age are not counted as such as long as she returns to work in the same unit. Similarly, the conditions surrounding pensions payable to agricultural production cooperative workers tended to favour women.

Equality of men and women is also recognized in civil and family law in both access to and exercise of those laws. Article 6 of the Natural and Juridical Persons Act states that "any civil juridical deed which would tend to restrain in any way the legal capacity of women, infringing upon the legal provision which sanction the full equality of women with men is entailed by nullity". An important general characteristic of the new regulations is the use of generic nouns or pronouns, such as person, wage earner and Romanian citizen, when referring to both men and women. Non-differentiation between the sexes is implicit in such laws.

The principle of full equality between men and women forms the basis of family law. Within marriage men and women have both equal rights and equal obligations. Assets accumulated during marriage become common property that may only be administered and disposed of by common consent, while assets obtained individually and prior to marriage may be disposed of by that person without reference to the spouse. Rights and duties of both partners to the marriage extend to their children, regardless of whether they are born outside the marriage or are adopted. Marriages may be dissolved, in exceptional cases, by divorce, at the request of either spouse taking into account the interests of any children. Both parents, regardless of who may be awarded custody of any children, are expected to contribute towards the expenses of rearing, education and professional training of those children.

Education, social and family situation

Women represent more than half of the population of Romania and over 41 per cent of the workforce. Almost half of the population live in rural areas. The industrialization and urbanization of the workforce required by economic development created favourable conditions for the improvement in the socioprofessional position of women in work, family and society. Such changes affect women's educational level and women's share of employment and women's willingness to work during maternity, all of which increased. Material conditions played an obvious role in those changes but so too did women's desire to participate in the process of development.

Elementary and secondary schooling in Romania is uniform and free of charge and is of 12 years duration. Higher education is provided by the State and includes universities and a number of private institutes. In the academic year 1985/86, 726,512 of the 1,492,654 pupils enrolled in forms V-VIII were girls, and 623,425 of the 1,226,927 pupils enrolled in forms IX-XIII were girls. For the same year university enrolment was 159,798, of which 71,658 or 44.84 per cent were girls. Of university graduates in 1989/90, women were most likely to hold a degree in the social fields, although 41.74 per cent of technical graduates were women.

The health of the population varies according to sex with women on average being healthier than men. The mortality rate is higher among men with the greatest difference recorded in the 16-64 age group where men are twice as likely as women to die. To safeguard and improve the health of the population the State has created a network of medical centres staffed by doctors and other health workers. In 1989 there existed a variety of hospitals, clinics, sanatoria and pharmacies including many that provided specialist services and treatment particularly maternal facilities and care for women. Family planning and abortion, essentially banned except in exceptional and approved circumstances, has been liberalized. Restrictive laws have been repealed and conditions favourable to the creation of a family-planning policy have been established.

The number of marriages in 1989 was higher than in 1988 and the majority of those who married were aged between 20 and 24 years and were marrying for the first time. Conversely, the divorce rate declined slightly, occurred most frequently among couples aged between 30 and 34 years, and in the majority of marriages dissolved the couple had dependent children. Women were more likely than men to be awarded custody of children upon divorce, thus single-parent families tended to be headed by women.

A network of crèches and kindergartens have been established in both rural and urban areas to assist mothers, particularly those employed by the State, in the rearing and supervision of children. The total number of children enrolled in 847 crèches in 1989 was 49,342 of whom 36,819 were enrolled on a daily basis and 12,523 on a weekly basis. Estimates from the Agricultural Production Co-operatives suggest that 31 per cent of children benefited from care and supervision in crèches and kindergartens.

Employment of women

The programme of economic development pursued by the Government resulted in the steadily increasing participation of women in the workforce. In 1985 women represented just below 40 per cent of the total workforce and in 1989 they represented over 41 per cent. In 1987 women represented 41.78 per cent of employees with higher education. The proportion of women in the various sectors of economic activity had grown annually. In 1989, women's percentage of employment in industry had risen from 26.5 in 1965 to 42.10; in commerce from 40 in 1965 to 72.9; in ready-made clothes from 87 in 1984 to 88.13 and in the textile industry from 74 in 1984 to 72.73. Women represented 58.25 per cent of the labour force involved in agriculture and approximately 200,000 women were working in education.

A large difference exists between the net annual income of women compared to that of men. More than 80 per cent of those who earn the lowest net income are women. In general, the percentage of women in a salary bracket increases as the salary decreases and vice versa. In the highest income brackets, even in industries traditionally dominated by women, women represent less than 2 per cent. In agriculture, the situation of women's wages is slightly better, with 65 per cent of those earning the lowest net salary being women, but the pattern is the same. Comparative data for the private sector are not available.

Women's organizations

The National Council of Women was abolished immediately after the revolution. Although no governmental women's organization exists, three non-governmental organizations were established recently: the Women's League of Romania, the Women's National Union of Romania, and the Women's Association of Romania. Each has its own platform and statute that provides particular ways of organizing and functioning but each is committed to the objective of the improvement of the status of women in all spheres, including employment and the family. Most importantly perhaps a level of competition between those groups has been observed which it is hoped may stimulate further activity. Activities of those organizations have included the establishment of scholarships to enable young women to continue their studies; sponsoring crèches; organization of excursions both within the country and abroad; cultural evenings; and the editing of their own newsletter. The National Union of Women of Romania, keen to organize a National Conference of Women, regularly publishes an independent magazine that provides information on all aspects of life and on the many roles of women. Radio and television provide little information for and about women and much of it is negative. Women's organizations, therefore, need to intensify their activities both among women and among the media to ensure that the voice of half the population and 41 per cent of the labour force is heard and heeded.

Trends and conclusions

The changes that occurred after the revolution of December 1989 that affected the status of women are divided into two categories: general reform intended to reestablish respect for human dignity and to guarantee fundamental freedoms and rights to all citizens; and women-specific reform intended to improve the status of women. Most important among those is the freedom to decide if and when to become a mother, access to family planning and the provision of paid leave for rearing a child until it is one year of age, and other problems and issues that affect women to a greater extent than men, especially women with young or many children. Particular attention was paid to health and social threats potentially posed by an increase in the incidence of such diseases as the acquired immuno deficiency syndrome (AIDS), the expansion of prostitution, the substantial drop in the birth rate and an increase in criminal activity among women, especially as it effects the status and well-being of women. Measures designed to prevent or limit such negative results of the recent changes in Romania should be undertaken by the State in order to consolidate and develop the advances already made in the improvement of the status of women in Romania.

B. Romania*

After 40 years of one-party totalitarian rule and 25 years of Ceausescu's dictatorship, Romania finally succumbed to internal pressures and joined the other countries of Eastern Europe in the process of transformation to a democratic society. The disintegration of Communist power was neither peaceful nor bloodless arising as it did from a population that was apathetic and severely repressed as well as extremely poor who daily witnessed the country's resources being squandered on useless programmes by a despotic ruler. The 15 months following the short but cruel civil war demonstrated that the process of change would continue to be particularly difficult and would affect everyone's lives, but would disadvantage women to a greater extent than men.

The situation in Romania can only be understood with reference to its history in which the public sector played a major role. A huge bureaucracy penetrated and controlled every aspect of social, public and private life. Individual freedoms and liberties had been suppressed for decades by the party-State, which ruled by force, intimidation and widespread control. The legal system under such conditions promoted a uniformity in all spheres of life: wages, education, representation in government and administration, minority rights and women's condition. At the same time, paradoxically, the State energetically promoted an equal-rights programme. A codex of laws entitled "The family codex" was introduced, which granted spouses equal rights and responsibilities. Women were encouraged to join the workforce and generally received comparable pay for comparable work. Women were represented in elected bodies, especially after 1970, in central and local governments and held leading positions based on a centrally established quota.

The past 40 years has also seen the disaggregation of schooling and access of girls to all educational institutions, including the traditionally male domains of metallurgy, naval engineering and the military police. Since 1950, the disparity between male and female enrolment in educational institutions has constantly decreased. Girls have gradually been catching up with boys in enrolment in primary education, have displayed better results in secondary and college enrolment and performance, and have considerably narrowed the gap in higher education.

Increased access to education has opened wider opportunities to women for employment. Although women have moved into traditional male areas of employment, they are predominant in such sectors as health care, where 75.4 per cent of all employees are women; education and cultural activities and arts, 68.2 per cent; retail trade, 62.5 per cent; and commercial activities, 62.5 per cent. In several manufacturing industries, mainly ceramics and chinaware, textiles, garments and footwear, their proportion greatly exceeds the national average. A number of professions have become strongly feminized, for

---

* by Mariana Celac, Group for Social Dialogue.

example, architecture and urban planning. Women graduated from a desegregated educational system only to join a highly segregated occupational structure.

Women receive comparable wages for comparable work and are guaranteed, by law, job security on marriage and throughout maternity. Fully paid maternity leave of four months followed by a further six months of reduced working hours to assist with breast-feeding is also guaranteed to women. Property rights, although restricted for every Romanian, are legally guaranteed regardless of marital status. A network of child-care institutions, although poorly equipped and inadequately staffed, were established, mostly during the 1970s when mass urbanization and industrialization drew large numbers of women into the workforce.

Policy relating to women's issues put into practice over the past 40 years provides a general legal framework of equality, bans wage differentiation on the basis of sex, promotes the emancipation of women by encouraging them into the labour force in large numbers and pursues a policy of compulsory representation of women in the decision-making process. Viewed in this way, and from the outside, the situation of women in Romania appears to be satisfactory. The results of the research recently completed by UNDP bear out this assumption. In the Human Development Index (HDI) all East European countries found themselves well placed as to "human development performance", with Romania ranked 90 of 130 countries on a table that combined life expectancy, adult literacy and purchasing power to arrive at an HDI value.

Nevertheless, something must have been profoundly wrong with the system in Romania for it to be so resolutely rejected and to collapse so rapidly . Something must also have been, therefore, profoundly wrong in the conditions of women and the philosophy underpinning their development. That philosophy was developed and perfected by Ceausescu. Two years after he came to power the party launched its ambitious industrialization programme accompanied by forced urbanization and the ill-famed "sistematizare" or demographic policy. A few years later, in the early 1970s, a general movement was initiated called the "minicultural revolution" by the Romanian intelligentsia, against human rights, individual freedom and creative independence.

The demographic policy, promulgated in 1967, comprised a package of laws that were swiftly passed through the Romanian National Assembly. A total ban was placed on abortion. Doctors risked prison and loss of license if caught performing an abortion and the patient faced a prison term. Emergency wards and operating rooms in gynaecological clinics were put under police surveillance. Approval from the State Attorney was required to perform a clinically justified abortion, and contraceptive devices and products were not available. Those measures were then periodically reinforced or extended. A quota of four children per family was imposed by law. Working women between the ages of 16 and 45 were subjected to compulsory examinations to detect non-declared pregnancies. Divorce became practically impossible to obtain. Justification for such actions lay in the falling birth rate and lax marital behaviour that was said to jeopardize the vigour and youth of the nation. Women had a patriotic duty to work, to procreate, to keep the family united and to educate the younger generation in a spirit of dedication, ethics and morality appropriate to a socialist society. The demographic policy, however, had been designed to sustain a level of development that ultimately led the country to economic disaster. Huge resources were committed to archaic, environmentally damaging industry and were taken away from health care and education; large numbers of people, particularly men, moved into the cities, crime rates rose and the sense of community dissolved in the urban areas.

The overall effects of the past decades on the situation of women are paradoxical:

(a) The great majority of women were regularly employed but in the name of equality they were required to work in sex-segregated labour. At the same time, as priority was given to the industrialization process, funding was not available to relieve the double burden of women;

(b) In rural collectivized areas women performed the hard labour but in non-collectivized areas women retained traditional roles within the family;

(c) Significant changes were achieved in skill and job distribution. Many highly skilled professional women, having taken advantage of equal opportunities in education, had successful careers in, for example, medicine, architecture, industrial design and education;

(d) Women were promoted to leading positions in party and administrative apparatus and were well represented in elected bodies, the party and the State hierarchy;

(e) An egalitarian approach to all social issues equalized wages, income and job opportunities. At the same time, shift work was maintained and part-time working arrangements and support facilities, such as day-care centres, were reduced. Women working in the textile, food-processing and construction industries were most affected by these changes;

(f) The demographic policy most affected women but its social toll, in illness, high infant mortality rate and personal suffering affected an entire generation and is yet to be accounted for.

Unlike other Eastern European countries or the Union of Soviet Socialist Republics, however, Romania had no period of *glasnost* or *perestroika* to stimulate intellectual debate on the future of reform or to allow the formation of a popular movement for change or to experiment with market economy strategies. Totalitarian rule abruptly ended in Romania and so began the complete transformation of the economy, of political structures of cultural and social arrangements. Economy, however, is the key to this process and a variety of economic measures were immediately initiated. Those were (a) stabilization, liberalization and macro-adjustment of the economic process; (b) privatization; (c) restoration of land; (d) establishment of a legal framework for structural change; (e) strengthened political support for privatization; (f) protection of the less able via a "safety net"; (g) convertibility of national currency; (h) reduction of inflation; (i) unemployment; (j) elimination of chronic shortages; (k) forming rational prices and (l) restoration of budgetary equilibrium.

The first 400 days of transition produced an outwardly depressing performance. Industrial marketable output and investment was less than two-thirds; exports were down by half and imports up by one eighth; productivity was down 30 per cent and unemployment grew alarmingly with between 120,000 and 200,000 people registered as out of work, and this is expected to rise in the medium term to 1.5 million. The economic situation was expected to deteriorate. The political and legal situation, particularly for women, has improved. The former Constitution and some of the most unpopular laws, including the one banning abortion, have been repealed. A multi-party political system has been installed and five months after the revolution elections were held and a number of groups, including youth, student and trade unions, became vocal in their demands for rapid and total change to the existing political and social arrangements. Unfortunately, Romania was also facing a number of new problems including the new alliances being made between the former hierarchy and the newly emerging businessmen; the growth of populist fundamentalism, rising xenophobia, ethnic conflicts and social clashes.

The reformation has particular implications for women and women's issues. It is expected that the framework of legislative and constitutional provisions concerning women's rights will not significantly change. At the same time, women's perception of emancipation is changing. Laws guaranteeing equal rights are no longer necessarily equated with equality of opportunity and new decisions on where and if to work are being made. Changed patterns of economic and political freedom have also led to a need to provide legal recognition, status and protection based on shifting ideas about the natural division of roles. At least a partial return of women to traditional roles within the family is foreseen as a result of the requirement for a more flexible economy and changed patterns of competitiveness. Among women themselves is a growing resentment against paid employment but this is less true among professional women who are developing new forms of economic activity including entrepreneurial endeavours.

The anticipated large increase in unemployment and rising prices is expected to adversely affect women. Many more women will become unemployed and the market philosophy underpinning the economic transformation will lead to a dismantling of the social-welfare programmes that protected women in the past. Moreover, the call to recover traditional values, attractive to both men and women, has led to many more women viewing child rearing as new and progressive. That maternal role is being idealized and encouraged, the more so as unemployment rises, as an alternative to maintaining women in the labour force. As privatization and free enterprise develops sharp differentiation in wages, income and wealth is expected, and already violence, prostitution and criminal activity are increasing. The use of the female body in advertising has increased and so has pornography and rape.

New forms of women's activism have developed in response to these changes but their issues tend to be absorbed by the overwhelming problems, such as political instability, economic crisis and ethnic conflicts, that are facing society as a whole. Although women continue to be in the forefront of intellectual and social resistance, their participation in the formal decision-making process is minimal. After December 1989, few women joined political parties or entered government. Few ran for or won parliamentary seats. In their quest for freedom and equality women appear to have rejected the formal mechanisms of power as manipulative and immoral. Women have returned to the essentially private sphere of the home, rejecting public life. Women must again become involved in civil society to ensure their equality.

C. Some aspects of the status of women*

Romania signed the tenth anniversary of its ratification of the Convention on the Elimination of All Forms of Discrimination against Women in 1980. After the 1989 revolution, it remains more committed than ever to the application of that Convention. A significant feature of the legislative reforms that have taken place in Romania in the post-revolution period is the constant effort to ensure that the law proclaims and guarantees all human rights recognized in United Nations instruments and at the Conference for Security and Co-operation in Europe. Those efforts are being made in spite of the difficult economic conditions that the Romanian Government, elected on 20 May 1990, has faced since coming to power. Their most important task, aside from fundamental political change, has been economic reform.

That reform has had unexpected social implications for all citizens, but in particular for women. Some of the important legislative measures that were undertaken during that period are: repeal or modification of existing laws in order to ensure respect for political and civil rights, in accordance with stated intentions and in adherence to international conventions on human rights; preparation of relevant studies and drafting of a new constitution; and coordination of national legislation with international standards.

Statistical data indicate that women constitute 50.7 per cent (11,786,844) of the total population but that they represent less than 49.9 per cent of the population aged 0 to 44, and more than 50 per cent of those aged 45 and over.

With regard to education, provisional data for 1990 indicate that girls represent 48.8 per cent of the population enrolled in pre-school institutions; 49.5 per cent of those attending primary schools; 53.6 per cent of those attending secondary schools; 34.4 per cent of students in trade schools; 8.5 per cent of those being trained as foremen/forewomen; 56.3 per cent of students pursuing a higher education and 47.2 per cent of students enrolled at university (38.3 per cent in technology; 59.0 per cent in medicine and pharmacology; 72.4 per cent in economics; 47.5 per cent in law; 60.3 per cent in education, and 43.9 per cent in arts).

Romanian women represent 45.2 per cent of the total work force (42.1 per cent in the industrial sector; 12.6 per cent in construction; 56.4 per cent in agriculture; 11.9 per cent in transportation; 53.4 per cent in telecommunications; 62.5 per cent in trade; 39 per cent in the service sector; 44 per cent in scientific research; 67.6 per cent in the teaching profession, arts and culture; 75.4 per cent in health and social assistance; 60.9 per cent in financial institutions and insurance concerns; 41.3 per cent in administration, and 37.6 per cent in other fields).

A crucial year in the change from a centralized socialist economy to a market economy was 1990. Laws enacted in 1990 (No. 31/1991: No. 15/1990: the law for landed property) on autonomous companies and commercial firms, and in 1991 on trusts, constituted important steps towards that end.

Economic changes have also resulted in unemployment. At the end of the first quarter of the present year, 9,689 of the 18,441 unemployed were women. In 20 departments the number of unemployed men was a little higher than that of women, but in 21 departments (including the capital) the number of unemployed women represented over 50 per cent of the total unemployed persons.

New ways of creating employment for women should be found that include developing those sectors where women have traditionally been employed, such as education, health and social assistance. Unemployment benefits should be raised in the case of women who have dependent children.

The participation rate of women in decision-making positions is disproportionate to that of men and is largely a result of a reaction against the past regulated promotion of communist women, often incompetent, to those positions.

That is true for all political parties. No woman, either from the government party or from any of the opposition parties, has attained a position higher than that of chief of a department. No women were found among the 23 ministers of the Romanian Government, and only one among the 59 Secretaries of State. The Commission in charge of drafting the new Constitution has no woman among its members. Within the regional executive organs, the highest position held by a woman is that of Vice-Prefect. That is also reflected in the representation of women in Parliament. Of 397 representatives, only 22 are women, and of 119 senators only 1 is a woman. Recently, parliamentary women have formed a group that will undertake the drafting of a proposal to adapt national legislation to international law.

---

*   by Irina Zlatescu, Deputy Director of the Romanian Institute for Human Rights, Law Professor, Academy for Economic Studies and Chairman, Romanian Association for Personal Liberty and Dignity of the Individual.

Non-governmental organizations dealing with women's issues are still attempting to define possible solutions to the problems encountered. In addition to working towards the improvement of the status of women and the elimination of all forms of discrimination against women, those organizations are seeking to facilitate access by women to modern forms of contraception. From 1 January 1990, the female birth rate (number of live births per 100 women aged 15 to 49) was 31.5 per cent.

It is difficult for women to participate in cultural activities, as most of their time is engaged in household shopping and other household tasks. It is believed that more publications addressing women's issues should be developed. Television is still State-controlled and family-oriented programmes are rarely offered.

To conclude, although Romanian legislation has recognized the right of women to participate in the political, economic and cultural life of the country, the participation of women in decision-making is not proportionate to education and employment levels. Women tend to remain at the lower or medium-level positions in decision-making. They also dedicate more time than men to the care of the family and the education of the children.

The Labour Code adopted in 1972 and modified after the December 1989 revolution, recognized equality of men and women in labour relations and provided for special measures for the protection of women in the labour force. Romanian law does not discriminate between men and women regarding family relationships (patrimonial or non-patrimonial). The new citizenship law proclaims the equality of men and women with regard to the citizenship of their children. The law does not distinguish between children born within or outside legal union. The penal and penitentiary law, which is to be modified with the assistance of experts from the Council of Europe, should probably take into consideration problems specific to mothers and women in special situations.

XI. UKRAINIAN SOVIET SOCIALIST REPUBLIC

A. The present situation of women*

Legal equality

Ensuring equality between women and men is a complex issue that depends on such factors as the economic potential of a country, the political will of its Government, the level of public consciousness and women's self-awareness, existing traditions and specific features of historical development. The complexity of women's interests and social functions should also be taken into account. The Constitution and the legislation of the Ukrainian SSR complied with article 2 (with the exception of paragraphs a, b, and f) and article 3 of the Convention on the Elimination of All Forms of Discrimination against Women as well as with a number of other international legal documents. During the reform process, however, the principles of equality and even the concept itself were distorted. The task of ensuring social rights, although here too a gap existed between legal norms and the de facto situation, took precedence over political and civil rights. The issue of improving the status of women was not given priority in the law-making activities of the Ukrainian SSR Supreme Soviet and not one of the many new laws was dedicated specifically to women's problems. Questions related to the status of women were being elaborated, however, in the preparation of long-term policy designed to upgrade the status of women in society.

At the union level, the role of the Supreme Soviet Commission in Charge of Women's Affairs, Family, Maternity and Childhood Protection was to ensure that the interests of women, families and children were reflected in laws adopted and to that end they drafted a number of normative documents that were examined by the Presidium of the Supreme Soviet. The Commission formulated a number of proposals and amendments on laws pertaining to labour, children's health and women's issues, including maternity. The documents considered were largely socially oriented, justified under conditions of economic crisis. The USSR Supreme Soviet Decree of 10 April 1990, on "Emergency Measures to Upgrade the Status of Women, Maternity and Childhood Protection, Consolidation of Family" was an important document intended to consolidate the social protection of working women that included measures to protect various vulnerable groups of women. The Decree is being implemented.

Economic reform and women's economic participation

There are 27.7 million women living in the Ukraine and they account for 54 per cent of the entire population of the Republic. Women in the Ukraine SSR as in the USSR as a whole have a high level of education and are engaged in a diversity of trades. More than 12 million women are employed. In 1989, 8 out of 10 able-bodied women worked and 7 out of 10 studied at the same time as they worked. Women accounted for 51 per cent of students enrolled in higher education and 57 per cent of those at technical secondary schools. Thirty per cent of workers trained at vocational schools were women. Over 4 million women had higher secondary or technical educational qualifications.

The aim of the State, for decades, has been to achieve quantitative equality between men and women. It is considered important that women should be represented in all categories of working people. Analysis, however, shows that numerous problems have accumulated as a result of that policy. There are notable disproportions in female employment. Despite women's educational achievement they account for more than half of the workers in jobs requiring unskilled manual labour. The principle of equal pay for work of equal value has become distorted. Mass employment of women in a national economy with an underdeveloped social infrastructure, and poor consumer services combined with traditional views of the responsibilities of men and women regarding housekeeping and child rearing have led to a physical and emotional overload among women. Such problems have been exacerbated during the course of *perestroika* by the protracted economic crisis that has been accompanied by the disintegration of the consumer market, price rises and shortages of commodities and food products, and women are increasingly threatened with unemployment as a result of economic reform.

Structure of female employment

In accordance with the Constitution, women and men have equal rights to education and professional training except in those trades that involve hard or harmful work wherein the training of women is prohibited or restricted.

---

* by Nina K. Kovalskaya, Ministry of Foreign Affairs.

The growth rate of female employment has slowed year by year as a result of measures aimed at stimulating the birth rate and the rearing of full employment of women. However, the extension of child-care services did contribute to an outflow of women from the labour force. Those women who are employed, however, have been increasingly employed in a wider range of industries. The feminization of certain branches of industry has decreased although women have dominated certain professions, for example, 75 per cent of cultural workers and 66 per cent of medical doctors are women. Women's share of the labour force has decreased in such fields as agriculture, forestry, textiles, and the food and tailoring industries but has increased in high-technology branches of industry such as machine-building, power engineering, chemistry and science.

Role of rural women in the new economic environment

More than 7 million rural women are engaged in agricultural production. Women account for almost 100 per cent of those employed in those agricultural branches, such as field husbandry, gardening and vegetable-growing, characterized by hard manual labour. Unfortunately, the critical state of the economy has not yet allowed labour conditions in those areas to be improved. The huge expenses incurred as a result of the accident at the Chernobyl nuclear power station hampered the implementation of social programmes. For those reasons legislative amendments designed to relieve rural women from manual labour have not been endorsed by the Ukrainian SSR Supreme Soviet. The amendment had been forwarded by the Commission in Charge of Women's Affairs. Rural women, however, enjoy a number of privileges, such as being pensioned regardless of age or seniority if they have five children and being provided for under the USSR Supreme Soviet Decree of 10 April 1990 that accorded priority development to rural areas. Economic reform aimed at the creation of new forms of employment has not been generally supported in rural areas.

Income distribution

The principle of equal remuneration for work of equal value was proclaimed in the Ukrainian SSR Constitution and in the labour code of the Republic. ILO Convention No. 100 "On Equal Remuneration of Men and Women for Work of Equal Value" has been ratified. In practice, however, women are paid less than men. Comparison of traditionally female branches of industry with traditionally male branches reveal a difference in wages of a ratio of 3 to 2. Almost one third of women earn less than 100 rubles per month compared with less than 2 per cent of men. More than 20 per cent of women with higher and specialized secondary education earn 100-120 rubles per month compared with only 7 per cent of men. The number of women who earn more than 400 rubles per month is almost four times lower than the number of men. The average monthly wage of women managers in industry is one third lower than that of men. Measures have been taken to improve the situation, such as increased wages in those branches of industry where women dominate the workforce, but the problem can only be solved by eliminating wage and salary differences in all areas of "female" labour.

Skill and job grading and professional qualification structures

The level of women's qualifications is much lower than that of men and is one of the major factors that affects their professional status and earnings. A system of continuous professional and economic training exists in the Republic and a number of training centres and workshops are being established. That is in accordance with the 1979 governmental decree on "Measures of the Further Perfection of Training and Upgrading Qualification of Workers in the Production Sphere". That decree provided the right to paid retraining and upgrading of qualifications for women who had children aged under 8 years. In practice, however, more than half of eligible women did not take advantage of that opportunity after marriage. In 1989 only 330,000 women underwent retraining or mastered new trades. Besides lack of spare time and tiredness, the reason women did not take advantage of those opportunities was that their professional status often remained the same despite the retraining.

Labour conditions

More than 3.3 million workers and collective farmers are engaged in manual labour. Of those, 408,000 women work in industry on a three- and four-shift schedule. Many thousands of women also work under harmful conditions. According to a survey conducted in 1990, every ninth woman estimates her labour conditions to be physically hard. A programme designed to restrict the use of manual labour is expected to relieve women of that situation. Analysis has shown that the 1986-1989 plan to improve the labour conditions and health of women succeeded and that the number of women working in conditions of excessive noise pollution and vibration and engaged in hard labour had been dramatically reduced. Due to the economic crisis such reductions slowed during 1990-1991. The period of transformation required new and radical changes of policy to ensure that the rights of working women were protected.

Unemployment, social security and social guarantee

Modernization of production processes and the transition to a market economy had led to a reduction of the labour force especially in those sectors engaged in unskilled manual labour, that is, those sectors dominated by women. Programmes of retraining of staff were instigated by all enterprises as part of the transition period to self-financing. Trade unions and women's councils also took part in those programmes. The Law on Employment of the Population, adopted by the Supreme Soviet of the Ukrainian SSR on 1 March 1991, contained State social guarantees of the right to work. The Law outlined special measures, including the reservation of 5 per cent of jobs at enterprises and organizations for people who required social protection, such as women who had young children and women of pre-pensionable age. Financial incentives were provided to organizations that employed in excess of that quota. A State employment service was established to implement the law and to organize professional training and retraining. Those registering at the employment service would receive grants of up to 75 per cent of their last average wage during the period of retraining. The law was both timely and important for managing labour problems arising from the transition to a market economy. The primary tasks faced by the Republic were to prevent the disintegration of the market, to devise a strategy to denationalize and privatize and to solve problems relating to ownership.

New forms of employment

Alternative forms of employment such as a reduced working day, cooperative agency employment, part-time employment and home-based employment, very attractive to women with young children, are not widely practised in the Ukraine. In particular, the development of the cooperative movement has opened up many opportunities for further female employment. The majority of the 800,000 people employed at cooperative agencies are women. Special requalification courses, however, are required for their effective operation and difficulties associated with the shortage of raw materials, equipment and poor legal protection have hampered the operation of the cooperative movement. The development of small businesses has also attracted great interest as a new form of employment for women.

Women's participation in decision-making processes

The right of women to actively participate in all areas - political, economic, social and cultural - relevant to the development of society is upheld in the Constitution of the Ukrainian SSR. Women have the right to vote upon reaching the age of 18 and have the right to stand for election to all bodies of power. No restriction, direct or indirect, to the exercise of those rights is allowed. Multi-mandate elections were held for the first time in 1987 and 1989. Various public organizations actively participated in that process as did many women. However, the results of those elections were hardly favourable to women. In the USSR Parliament the share of women decreased from 33 per cent in 1984 to 16.6 per cent in 1989. In the Supreme Soviet of the Ukrainian SSR, women accounted for only 13 of 450 deputies or 2.8 per cent of deputies, compared with 36 per cent in 1984. The number of women represented at the regional level also decreased, accounting for only 7 per cent of deputies elected to the regional Soviets. Women were not represented at the level of chairperson or deputy chairperson of the regional Soviets nor as chairpersons of the regional executive committees. There was only one woman among the selected Ministers, and she was the Minister of Social Security. Only 5.3 per cent of the high-ranking leaders of enterprises and organizations were women. The results of the elections demonstrated that stereotypes of women's ability to lead still exist. Women are not yet prepared for a political struggle and they are unable to defend their constitutional rights in that area.

The process of democratization, however, which highlighted women's problems and placed the issue of the status of women squarely on the political agenda, has created favourable conditions to the solution of the "women's" question. Women have begun to take a more active part in the social and political processes, and the number of new women's organizations has grown and the scope of their activities has increased. Those organizations include the Committee of Soldiers' Mothers, the Association of Businesswomen and the Association Koliska. Also very active are the women's section of the People's Movement Rukh, the Green World Association and the Ukrainian Language Society. A Commission on Women's Affairs has also been established under the Central Committee of the Communist Party of the Ukraine and the Women's Council of the Ukraine has been developing new activities to attract more support. The expansion of the activities of those organizations and consolidation of their role in solving social problems should improve women's self-awareness and improve their chance for success in future election campaigns.

Enlarging the role of women in society, however, depends on the level of activity and degree of authority of the national mechanism that works out and coordinates policy relating to the status of women. Work on creating such a mechanism in the Ukraine has not yet been completed. Although the Supreme Soviet Commission in Charge of Women's Affairs, Family, Maternity and Childhood Protection is functioning, no corresponding body has been established within the top executive body, the Council of Ministers. The absence of such a mechanism hampers the establishment of other coordinating ministries and departments and the development of cooperation between the Commission and scholars who specialize in the study of women's problems. Ultimately, the long-term programme to up-grade the status of women has been delayed.

Policy changes relating to the role of women and men in society

According to the 1989 census there were 14.1 million families in the Ukraine of which almost two-thirds had two or three members, 25 per cent had four members and 14 per cent had five or more members. Of women aged 16 and older, 12 per cent had never married compared with 18 per cent of men. The birth rate has been dropping. Over the past two decades the number of divorces and single parent families, usually headed by a woman, has increased. Women face increased difficulties in combining their functions of mother and worker with their public activities. In compliance with the USSR Supreme Soviet Decree of 10 April 1990, the State provided working mothers and other vulnerable groups, including heads of incomplete families, young mothers and the disabled, with special support and protection. Those measures include increased maternity leave and benefits; increased assistance to mothers aged less than 18 years; a revised list of production fields, trades and other work considered hard or harmful that was prohibited to women and teenagers; revised regulations governing the performance night-shift work by women, particularly those with young or invalid children; and increased monthly allowance to single mothers. The network of pre-schools was expanded and housing was provided to those who required it. To further consolidate the family, increase parental responsibilties, consolidate children's rights, and protect maternity and childhood, amendments were introduced to the Matrimony and Family Code, the Housing Code and the Civil Code of the Republic.

Unfortunately, all those measures are insuffi-

cient to solve the problems faced by women. Women are overloaded due to family responsibilties and an underdeveloped social and consumer services infrastructure. According to a number of studies, women's work load at home exceeds that of men by 2-2.5 times. Women spend 3 hours a day on house-keeping and 7-8 hours a day at the weekend. Little time is left for child rearing. That situation has contributed to the instability of families and could only be solved by changing people's, particularly young people's, attitudes towards family responsibilities, including the rearing of children. The active participation of the mass media would assist in that endeavour.

Maternity and childhood protection

The past two decades have seen a change in the demographic pattern in the Ukraine. In six regions of the Ukraine the mortality rate surpassed the birth rate. The mass involvement of women in productive activity contributed to the decline in the birth rate. The situation has been aggravated by the ecological crisis and the lack of resolution of problems relating to maternity and childhood. Harmful production factors combined with harmful environmental factors has caused ecologically dependent ailments among pregnant women, mothers who breast-feed their babies and young children. To improve that situation the Government adopted a number of measures including the approval of the "Comprehensive Program of Ailment Prevention and Formation of a Healthy Mode of Life of the Ukrainian SSR Population for the Period up to the Year 2000"; the development and approval of the concept of protection of the genetic fund of Ukraine's population; new regulations governing conditions at health-improvement establishments for children and on the construction of sanatoria for children were approved. Also, a number of policy changes were made in the area of child and maternal health, including the provision of medical and genetic assistance to the public; prevention of childhood disability; development of special medical aid to women and children; and the provision of baby food in ample quantities.

B. The impact of economic and political reforms on the status of women*

Legal equality

The first Constitution of the Ukrainian SSR, drafted in 1919, incorporated the concept of equality between men and women. New Constitutions and amendments further consolidated the principle of equality in political, social, economic and cultural

spheres. Thus the women's question was considered solved. Women were accorded equality with men in education and training; in public, political and cultural life; in employment, earning and career development, with special measures to regulate working conditions designed to facilitate the combination of labour and maternity; and legal protection, financial

---

* by Valentina Zlenko, Institute for Social and Economic Problems of Foreign Countries, Ukrainian Academy of Sciences.

and moral support of maternity and childhood was also provided.

As time went by, however, the progressive nature of women's involvement in society was undermined by changed social practices and perceptions of women's roles. Legal equality had been accorded to women but a gap developed between that and their de facto equality. The recent economic, social and political changes have given impetus to a re-examination of that situation, both actual and legal. The Constitution, however, does not embody such rights as the right to life, the right to protection from interference in private life and the right to protection from violence in the family. Women as individuals are not guaranteed the right to exercise and enjoy fundamental freedoms and human rights.

During its sessions in 1990-1991, the Ukrainian Parliament considered many new bills. Not one of them was dedicated to women's problems although the interests of women were taken into account during debates on such issues as tax law and the land code. Changes were also made recently to the labour law especially as it applied to women during periods of maternity and to families with children. The legislation also made provision for new forms of employment. Other proposed amendments, including the reduction of the working day to six hours for women with children under the school age with no loss of salary, were rejected on the basis of economic difficulties. Women were often exploited or discriminated against in their place of employment but no legal provisions were made to discourage practices such as sanctions against offending persons, organizations or enterprises. Many women worked under difficult, hazardous or unhealthy conditions although it was prohibited to employ them under those conditions.

Woman's role as mother was considered a priority area of women's issues. The family was regarded as the most stable structure of modern society and its effective functioning should be encouraged. Women's productive activity should not be at the expense of their reproductive function. The existing system of social support to mothers was inadequate and required many changes to improve the status of women. For real and lasting change in the status of women to occur existing customs, practices and stereotypes of women's roles that had given rise to discriminatory practices against women should be modified or abolished. The necessary economic and social conditions should also be established to ensure both de facto and de jure equality of women and men. That will be neither a short nor a simple task.

Economic reform and women's economic participation

With reference to official statistics, trade-union information and sociological research from 1980 to 1990, the evolution of women's status and the changes that have occurred as a result of the economic reforms could be observed. Analysis of such information showed that women had been broadly integrated into the process of economic development but that that integration was irregular, fluctuating according to the health of the economy. Of the 27.7 million women in the Ukraine in 1989, 10.6 million of them were engaged in some form of economic activity, a drop from 10.8 million in 1986, before the economic reforms began and the point at which female employment apparently peaked. Women still accounted for 52 per cent of the labour force and that had remained stable over the past decades despite a slight drop in their total share of the population from 55 per cent in 1970 to 54 per cent in 1989. Women's participation in the labour force had gradually and inexorably increased, largely due to social and economic necessity. In times of economic crisis women's participation in the labour force was necessary either as the major source of income for them and their families or as a second income, equally necessary for survival. At the same time, women's position in the labour force was less favourable than men's at such times and extra efforts were required to mitigate the disadvantages they suffered. Resources, however, were obviously limited to ameliorate the situation during times of economic crisis. Women also worked, however, for personal reasons. Work provided moral and personal satisfaction for women and allowed them to exercise their knowledge and talents. But work also was dysfunctional for women as it did not create conditions conducive to combining that function with mothering.

The level of economic development has a significant effect on the economic role and status of women. The sectoral and industrial structure of female employment has changed in accordance with changes in the total labour-force structure as a response to changing economic requirements. The service sector, for example, accounted for 26.4 per cent of the total labour force in 1989 compared with 24 per cent in 1986. Most of that increase occurred in low-level management. As women were concentrated in the service sector they accounted for much of that increase. Women accounted for 85 per cent of persons employed in trade and public catering; 80 per cent in health and social security; 75 per cent in education; and 72 per cent in culture and art. Women's employment was concentrated in a number of non-farm branches of industry. Women accounted for over 45 per cent of persons employed in manufacturing; almost 30 per cent in the building industry; and in textiles, mechanical engineering, instrument making and the radio industry women accounted for more than 70 per cent of employees. Women's share of employment in the agricultural sector, although decreasing, remained high and it was expected that women's employment in the developing private sector would increase. The employment of women in some traditionally male spheres, such as agriculture, and jobs, such as engineers and economists, had increased but women remained strongly underrepresented in senior administrative and managerial jobs and in most academic and scientific occupations. The labour market on the whole remained segregated along male and female jobs and was largely characterized by decreased horizontal occupational segregation but static vertical segregation. Women's employment was limited by traditional perceptions of women's roles but tended to be concentrated in industries and occupations with bad working conditions, night work, manual work and low levels of responsibility.

Rural women face particular employment difficulties. More than 7 million women live in rural areas of the Ukraine and of those 3.5 million are working in various farm-based industries. Among collective farmers they account for 49 per cent in 1980 and 45 per cent in 1989. Almost 100 per cent of the labour force engaged in field-cropping, vegetable growing and gardening are women. Dairy farming, the most labour intensive sector of farming is largely "female". Women employed in that field are twice as likely as other women to suffer physical and other health problems particularly related to maternity. The level of health and medical care, including access to information, counselling and family-planning services, available to rural women is generally poor. The recent organization of self-help groups and cooperative and other agrarian reforms has increased only minimally the protection of women, and other problems, such as housing, sanitation, electricity and water supply, transport and communication, have not been solved. According to a recent referendum, 15 per cent of the people surveyed intend to leave the collective farms and work on their own, while 40 per cent want to work by family contract within a collective farm. More than 26 per cent of the people surveyed considered that collective farms should remain the main form of economic activity, 11 per cent preferred the farm and 36.7 per cent thought that all economic activity was valid. Of rural people, 23 per cent preferred the concept of private property compared with 27 per cent who preferred the collective farm arrangement. Almost 80 per cent of the people interviewed were dissatisfied with contemporary rural life because of bad living conditions, low payment and a perceived dismissal of the rural worker's opinion.

More than 1 million people in the Ukraine also work under unhealthy or difficult conditions. Many women are employed at heavy jobs in an atmosphere of high noise and vibration that is poorly lit. Between 20 and 50 per cent of female labour positions fall short of norms and rules of labour protection prohibiting them from working under such conditions. Many industries that largely employ women lack even basic forms of mechanization and automization. Although women are entitled to receive various

privileges and compensation for working under such conditions, many do not. Many women are employed in night work although it is prohibited except as a "temporary measure" (that temporary measure has existed for 70 years) but as modern production techniques often require night work for efficiency, facilities and working conditions should be improved. They should also be improved for reasons of health. Fortunately it is gradually being recognized that a medical-biological approach to the health of working women was inadequate and that the environmental factors are also important. However, responses to the problems of women's employment and working conditions have so far been fragmented, low key and have generally ignored their economic foundation. An administrative solution is both illusory and harmful to women and should be replaced by a policy designed to eliminate the economic basis that determines those conditions.

Discrimination against women remains in the wages they receive. Despite formal juridical recognition of the principle of equal payment for work of equal value contained in the Ukrainian Constitution and other official documents, a gap exists between payment made to men and that made to women. The average wage of a woman employed in industry is 70.9 per cent of that of a man; in building trades it is 62.5 per cent; and in transport it is 72.2 per cent. On average in all fields women's wages are 54.7 per cent of those received by men.

A study undertaken in the Ukraine in 1989 found that more than 15 per cent of women received less than 90 roubles per month compared with approximately 2 per cent of men, but that only 1 per cent of women received more than 400 roubles per month compared with more than 10 per cent of men. Education had a bearing on wages received. The average wage received by women with higher education was between 160 and 180 roubles compared with 250 to 300 roubles received by men with higher education. Conversely, 20.2 per cent of women holding higher and special secondary education received the lowest wages compared with only 6.9 per cent of men.

Changes in the economy accompanied by the development of science and technology also demand an increasingly qualified labour force. The qualification of all workers should increase. Women's qualification level remains lower than men's despite the fact that the percentage of women among specialists with higher and special secondary education is 61.6 per cent. Across industry, four times as many women as men are found in the low skill category of employment and only 3.6 per cent of women have undergone special training to improve their qualifications. For many women, however, increased qualifications do not lead to promotion at work. The opposite experience is true for men. No new training programmes have been instigated, however, and no information is available on how that could be achieved and how existing social guarantees and protection for women would be maintained. Despite educational advantages, improvement of qualifications is much more difficult for women than for men as women largely have responsibility for children and the home in addition to their waged employment and consequently have no time for professional development.

Similarly, career development poses difficulties to women as vertical occupational segregation is found both between and within occupational categories. The latter occurs where women and men have the same occupation but are employed at different levels of responsibility and allocated different tasks. Difficulties associated with the professional training and qualification of women are exacerbated by the existence of a barrier to their vertical mobility. According to official data, the number of women who head State-owned enterprises of different sizes is 309,700 of whom 74 per cent are appointed and 26 per cent are elected to the position. Most women departmental heads are concentrated in industry, trade, the information sector, transport and science. In female-dominated industries, such as education and health care, women account for between 16 and 28 per cent of heads of branches. New possibilities for career development exist. Provided the State provides legal protection and economic support women could demonstrate their business qualities as heads of small businesses and cooperatives.

Participation in the decision-making processes

Women are accorded full political equality in the Constitution but the democratization process has increased their scope for initiative and opportunity to participate in the process of reorganization. Originally women were among the strongest supporters of *perestroika* but that optimism has given way to uncertainty, confusion and pessimism. One third of women see some positive improvement in public life but most consider the status of women to be worse than before. The democratization process also affects women's voting and election behaviour. They have a wide range of political views that are independently formed and exercised at elections. Their political activity has increased considerably, as witnessed by their interest shown in the 1987 and 1989 election campaigns, but is still less than that of men. The reform of the political system and the new election law have had mixed consequences for women: the quota system of representation has been abolished and women's representation in parliament has dropped to half its previous level; the status of women is sufficiently low that both women and men vote for male candidates; the higher the level of government the smaller the representation of women.

In the Ukraine Supreme Soviet only 2.8 per cent of deputies are women while 7 per cent of those in regional Soviets are women. There are no women among chairmen of Regional Soviets, their deputies and chairmen of Regional executive committees. Women account for only 5.3 per cent of leaders of enterprises and organizations. The 27.7 million women living in the Ukraine are not well represented. The reasons for the low level of participation by women are complex but connected to the generally low status of women in society, difficult working conditions and high level of family responsibility. Specifically, women deputies, unlike men, tend to lack the required knowledge and training for State activity. Women are not prepared in any way to become leaders or to participate in governmental activities. And those women who are often emulate a masculine command style that has contributed to negative attitudes towards female leaders.

Women's participation in other forms of political actions, non-governmental organizations and associations has also increased. Approximately 40 per cent of women have demonstrated potential readiness to take an active part in social protest and 5 per cent of women have already done so. The process of democratization created new and revived old public organizations such as women's councils. The main activities undertaken by the councils are care of the family, improvement of working conditions for women, improvement of the social sphere. Unfortunately, the councils tend to be ineffective and do not involve the mass of women. Women are more active in the movement for the reform of the armed forces. A Congress of Soldiers Mothers took place in 1990 at which the women expressed many demands, both social and military.

In summary, women appear to be largely absent from decision-making positions although their political activity has increased. The prestige of leading positions and the privileged life of the governmental elite has created a "closed shop" run by men to which women are not easily admitted. Insufficient attention has been paid to the advancement of women in governmental bodies and their professional advancement has been largely ignored and limited by traditional stereotypes of women's roles and functions. That has also given rise to the double burden many women carry at the work-place and at home that in turn reduces available time for professional upgrading. Professional training for leadership positions is generally not available to women and the mechanism to promote women in governmental bodies is also absent.

Policy changes relating to the role of women and men in society, especially sharing domestic and parental responsibilities

The family has significantly evolved over the past 20 years. People marry younger and the number of incomplete families has risen. The birth rate, the number of families without children, the number of children born by single women and the number of divorces have all risen. The mass involvement of women in the labour force has resulted in their increased independence that has brought about new functions for them while maintaining their traditional ones. Increased economic independence of women has contributed to the furtherance of their equality with men. The new economic conditions, however, have intensified the difficulty of combining work, public activity and maternal duties. Although the State has made a considerable effort during the 1970s and 1980s to increase and broaden the forms of social assistance available for families, that effort has proved insufficient. The status of the family has deteriorated in the past five years of economic crisis and many economic, social, demographic and moral problems faced by them remain unsolved. Women especially experience difficulties as they are largely responsible for the performance of a variety of home duties that are usually performed without the assistance of machinery. Home labour is also unremunerated and is thus devalued in the social consciousness. At the end of her waged working day a woman can expect to work at least a further three hours at home. Women work from 2 to 2.5 times more hours than men do in the home. Women's expansion into the labour market is not accompanied by changes in the traditional division of labour within the family. Men participate minimally if at all in the rearing of children and in the performance of housework. Given the feminization of certain spheres of employment, such as in kindergartens and schools, men exert little or no influence on children and younger generations and thus the traditional models persist. In recent years, the Government has taken certain steps to increase the rights of fathers to care for their children but that is both limited in application and of minimal value in changing peoples perceptions of traditional male and female roles.

According to the 1989 census, there are 14.1 million families and 15 million children in the Ukraine. The population is decreasing but the number of families with one or two children is stable. Chernobyl caused particular health and social problems that required an immediate and large response that drew resources away from other forms of social funding. During the period of economic crisis the most vulnerable groups in society were female heads of households, mothers of large families and children. Although a State system of family support is in place it is insufficient to deal with current problems. The form of the system is also inadequate and should be changed to allow indexation of benefits in the face of rising inflation, and payments should be increased to the level of the minimum wage for women at home caring for children. Family planning has also become an issue of increased importance particularly to women. Until now, no State system of family planning has been elaborated, nor have the issues involved even been discussed. All forms of contraceptives are largely unavailable. Families have been largely autonomous and self-reliant in terms of decisions regarding the bearing and rearing of children and new measures should be designed to facilitate not limit that form of development. Families should be encouraged to material independence through the provision of credits and loans to establish small business, to build or buy a house.

XII. UNION OF SOVIET SOCIALIST REPUBLICS

A. Socio-economic changes and the position of women*

The Union of Soviet Socialist Republics has undergone radical changes, regarded by some as a revolution and by others as modernization, the effects of which have been felt in all spheres of society: political, economic and social. Although the effects of the restructuring process have been felt in every stratum and group in the population, they have not been evenly spread. Women appear to have been the most adversely affected during this transition period particularly when compared to men. Recognition of this has been slow as notions of social equality are largely outside of public and political consciousness.

Before analysing the specific aspects of women's situation, however, it is useful to note three major trends. Political changes have led to a reduction in the number of women in formal decision-making structures but to a rise in general political activity and the appearance of independent women leaders. A movement for a woman president is gathering momentum. The economic sphere has witnessed on the one hand increased unemployment among women, as the "second grade" work-force, and on the other hand the formation of an independent group of women entrepreneurs. Social changes have been observed in the increasingly feminization of poverty and social stratification along gender lines. Thus, although the current situation of women arose in part from the general crisis experienced in the USSR, it was also attributed to the persistence or resurfacing of traditional attitudes towards the "weaker sex". Questions concerning the future role of women have been considered within the context of the articles of the Convention on the Elimination of All Forms of Discrimination against Women and the Nairobi Forward-looking Strategies.

Legal equality of women and the pattern of their political participation

Despite a paucity of statistical data on the political involvement of women, some generalizations can be drawn from the information available. Although women have always been active in formal public work, in general, little political activity has been observed. That can be explained partly by the existence of traditional stereotypes that identify politics as a male domain, and give rise to resistance to political aspirations of women, as well as exclude women from important informal networks. A number of factors, however, have also limited women's political activity. Although no specific legislation has

prevented women from participating in political structures, a number of acts, by reinforcing traditional stereotypes, indirectly discriminate against women. For example, some codes provide that women, rather than parents, need to be assisted in combining parental functions with remunerated work. A woman is viewed as a worker having special advantages who is thereby not reliable enough to move up the structure of administrative and political power.

The absence of a practical political strategy, either formal or informal, aimed at increasing women's involvement combined with the nominal inclusion of women in the power structure via the formal quota system has resulted in the estrangement of women from real political activity and the confinement of that activity into a formal network of women's councils that have been organized from above. The restructuring process saw a partial lifting of this quota system and as a result women's representation in legal and executive bodies fell from 33 to 17.5 per cent. The electoral system based on single-member districts for election worked against the election of women. There were positive factors for the future in women's full employment in the labour force, their share of education and the growth of pluralism in politics.

Statistics on women's membership of and participation in new political parties, professional organizations and other types of political activity are not available. Although the new period of democratization and openness and political pluralism witnessed the birth of many new political, social and trade-union groups, social equality and women's rights are not on the agenda or are interpreted according to traditional, patriarchal values or social cost/benefit analysis. Where statistics do exist on women's participation in political groups, it has been found that they are more likely to join those parties, such as the Green Party and the Blue Movement (For Social Ecology of Human Beings), concerned with global problems such as ecology, human rights and nuclear war. Even there women are not adequately represented in the decision-making structures even though they are extremely active members. Within the trade-union movement, however, the increasing marginalization of women's labour, their uncertain economic status and the threat of unemployment have resulted in an increased number of women becoming active members.

*   by Natalia Rimachevskaya, Director, Institute for Socio-Economic Studies on Population, USSR Academy of Sciences.

The transition period saw the unofficial women's movement (approximately 50 women's groups and associations are currently registered in Moscow) exploring possibilities for political participation, examining the role of women in society and slowly developing ideas of social equality. The lack of information and strict censorship during the period of existence of the Soviet State; the low level of public awareness of women's issues; and the lack of confidence among women rendered even the imagining of emancipation difficult. Women's groups tend to be fragmented, and lacking unity of purpose, theory and organization. They incorporate many different philosophical backgrounds and, although their goals are the same, their methods for achieving equality for women are varied. The increasing involvement of women in such organizations has the potential to effect great change, to increase confidence, to stimulate discussion based on notions of social equality between men and women, to heighten public awareness of those issues, and to inform and formulate policy that affects women and the political involvement of women. Although women have become increasingly involved in political processes, no one party or organization adequately expresses women's interests; and women's political consciousness and involvement is still at a lower level than that of men.

Economic reform and women's employment

Women comprised 53 per cent of the population of the USSR in 1989. Their level of employment was one of the highest in the world but both their labour force participation and their share of the total labour force fluctuated according to the state of the economy. The industrialization of the 1930s was accompanied by a massive flow of women into the productive process. Their participation peaked during the Great Patriotic War, decreased in the post-war period, increased in the 1970s, and again decreased during the transition period (1985-1990). Their involvement was not stable across republics, which was attributed to higher birth rates and larger families in some areas. Women were mobilized when labour was scarce and returned to "the fold of the family" when it was in abundance. Traditionally, scant attention has been paid to the needs or desires of women themselves. Their labour could be characterized as "compensating" material.

Women's employment has also been distributed unevenly across industries and trades. Women's employment is concentrated in jobs in the social infrastructure and some industries, such as trade and public catering; and health, physical culture and services have become "feminized", resulting in low status and low wages. Some 300,000 women are engaged in hard manual labour in industries such as wood-working, pulp and paper and polygraphic industries, where conditions are described as difficult, hazardous and especially hazardous. Working conditions in agriculture are even worse and women comprise 80 per cent of the 60 per cent engaged in manual labour. In 1989, the share of women performing manual work in industry was 43 per cent (26 per cent for men), in construction 79 per cent (44 per cent men) and in agriculture 79 per cent (55 per cent for men). Yet wide-scale resistance on the part of women to attempts to transfer them to other jobs has been noted, because of the special conditions associated with hazardous work. The reasons cited by the women include, in addition to higher wages, early retirement possibilities, prolonged leave and shorter working hours. Unfortunately, an analysis has revealed that people employed in those areas would be least mobile and least capable of adjusting to the changes wrought in the transition to a market economy and would have a higher likelihood of unemployment.

Women's work, however, has not been confined to paid employment. Traditional patriarchal attitudes towards work have resulted in a sexual division of labour that has allocated the role of homemaker to women. Such attitudes are used to justify the "double employment" of women. On average the total weekly working hours of a woman, professional and home chores, are 76.3 compared with only 59.4 for men. Studies reveal a high level of fatigue and dissatisfaction with their current job among women who combine work and family duties. In one study, 40 per cent of the women surveyed desired to change their job. The most important reasons given were free working hours, higher wages, closer proximity of work to home and better working conditions. Creative work and career development were not considered as important. Compared with men, women are less likely to attend courses to raise their skills or to retrain in a second profession. Such courses tend to be oriented towards men's professions.

This "duality" of women's work has also led to a mismatch between women's educational level and level of employment and remuneration. Although the percentage of women having higher education increased 19 points between 1979 and 1989, compared with an increase of 13 for men, and first-time women employees had a higher level of education than men, women still tend to hold jobs requiring less skill and with fewer opportunities for promotion than men. Despite the concept of equal labour remuneration regardless of sex the women receive, on average, wages that are, one-third lower than those received by men. Of women with higher or specialized secondary education only 7 per cent are engaged in managerial work compared with 48 per cent of men. Women are basically not represented in the higher echelons of power, in international relations and in the advanced fields of science and technology. Women professionals average wages 3-4 points below those of men and women are minimally involved in managerial activities. The feminization of particular jobs or industries is characterized by low wages, low status and few opportunities for promotion.

Although the restructuring process witnessed the removal of the barrier of rigid party hierarchy connected with the system of administrative-command management, it revealed the previously hidden barrier of gender. An ideology of social protectionism towards women exists and is justified in terms of women's unique reproductive function. Women form a special, specific work-force because of that role and should be protected from hazardous work as well as encouraged in the performance of domestic duties. Shorter working hours, maternity leave and the granting of free days for domestic duties are all provided as incentives to reduce the participation of women in productive activities. As women are often viewed as "second workers" it also provides justification for their relatively lower wages. The more women are "protected" as mothers the more they are marginalized in employment.

The new economic reforms, in addition to changing the type of production, will have a different system of financing and presuppose the need for profitability. If women are protected as mothers they will be marginalized as having too high a potential cost to an enterprise. Transition to a market economy has increased the risk of redundancies as the effects of privatization and reconstruction are felt in increased demands for a skilled and professional work-force. It is not surprising, therefore, given the existing vulnerability of the female labour force, that women are among the first to be made redundant. Of the employees made redundant during the 1985-1987 "reduction of management apparatus", more than 80 per cent were women. Of those people who have lost their jobs in the last two years, 60 per cent are women.

The female labour force is being increasingly characterized as low-skilled and non-creative, having access to a limited range of professions and working under poor conditions with minimal professional mobility for appreciably lower wages. Their risk of redundancy is high. Thus it could be expected that more and more women would lose the social protection that came from employment, such as pensions, partially paid child-care leave and the possibility of shorter working hours, and that the process of the feminization of poverty would increase.

Participation in decision-making

The level of women's participation in decision-making is an important indicator of the degree of achievement of genuine equality. Although women have always been active in voluntary organizations, their level of participation in formal decision-making processes in socio-political activities is low and far less than that of men. The period of restructuring has

seen their formal participation decrease further with their share among deputies of the USSR Supreme Soviet falling from 33 to 15.6 per cent. Women are largely absent among leaders of the new public organizations, and often few in number among members. Existing political and administrative bodies are not prepared to admit the participation of women on an equal basis with men.

Although there are no legal barriers to women's participation in decision-making, traditional stereotypes and attitudes limit their participation. The combination of productive and reproductive roles leaves little time for political activities let alone managerial ones. Women's biological potential and the privileges attached to that render her unreliable for promotion within administrative or political structures. The absence of both a coordinated women's movement and a genuine political desire to achieve social equality are also important factors in explaining the absence of women in decision-making. To ensure the equal representation of women in decision-making positions those barriers must be overcome.

Formal quotas have been discredited so new strategies have to be devised. For example, if the share of women in the leadership of a given organization is less than their share among the employees in that organization then a policy of preferential treatment could be pursued. Such a strategy could also be incorporated into collective bargaining agreements, making the receipt of special funding dependent upon them pursuing a policy of preferential treatment and channelling those funds into political and managerial training programmes for women employees. The creation of an independent genuine women's movement is an *a priori* condition to women's participation in decision-making.

Measures necessary to solve women's problems

The situation of women in the USSR evidently requires an urgent response. Special measures for the social protection of women should be put in place, and traditional stereotypes and attitudes about the appropriate roles and duties of men and women within the family and society should be challenged. To this end, a decision was taken by the Parliament on 14 April 1990, which contained a number of provisions for women. The principal ones were: increased allowances for rearing children up to the age of 18 months, equivalent to the minimum wage; fully paid maternity leave for 56 days prior to and 70 days after birth; and non-paid parental leave up to three years granted to the mother or, at the discretion of the family, the father or other relative. Those provisions were a beginning but should be elaborated to include others aimed at improving women's employment opportunities: institution of a system of the professional re-education of women after their return to work from child-care leave; special courses aimed at skill improvement for women who have children; revision of procedures of hiring and promotion of women; and stimulation of investments for the improvement of working conditions for women. To be effective, those measures should be extended and differentiated with regard to different regions and enterprises as well as newly emerging problems. A number of organizations are already in the process of working out such programmes.

Further special measures are required to neutralize the negative consequences for women of the development of a two-sector model of the labour market. Unemployment and a division-of-labour market along progressive and traditional lines often accompanied that type of intensive reform. Women, because of their role as mothers and carers, were more likely to be relegated to the second or traditional sector that was characterized as low-paying, low-status and holding little potential for advancement. Those measures could include legislative acts that oblige an organization to employ a particular percentage of women and ensure that women comprise no more than 50 per cent of workers made redundant. More importantly, efforts should be directed towards making gender a neutral factor when considering the economic interests of an organization. These would include measures aimed at minimizing the cost to employers of employing women by providing, for example, tax rebates to the organization to compensate for expenditure on child-care, kindergartens and leave to care for sick children. One proposal is to set aside a share of profits (a "child factor" that would be based on the ratio between the number of children of the workers of a given enterprise and the total number of employees) to be used to provide funds for these support services to parents of either sex.

Entrepreneurship, cooperative forms of organization of production and individual labour activities also require particular attention to ensure women's labour does not become marginalized or redundant. Special retraining programmes and labour legislation are required to ensure the equality of opportunity in employment; and cultural and educational methods should be developed aimed at breaking down existing stereotypes on and attitudes to the division of male and female roles. The idea of parenthood as a joint responsibility should be developed. Only then may it be possible for a competitive and active female labour force to emerge, based on principles of equality.

Changes in family policy including family planning and parenthood

Families are encountering many problems. Economic difficulties combined with poor services, imperfect civil legislation and a large and unwieldy bureaucratic apparatus, all contribute to the difficult situation many families find themselves in. Problems are often particularly acute when a young couple is considering having children. High child mortality, the deterioration of women's health and the unsatisfactory functioning of medical institutions are the main problems connected with motherhood. Access to child-care is another. Pre-school care is the most controversial and largely insufficient, with some 2 million children requiring places at kindergartens and crèches.

Abortion is a major issue in women's health. Although there has been a reduction in the number of abortions performed in recent years, the USSR holds a leading position in the world for the number of abortions performed. Abortion has become the dominant method of birth control as information, medical assistance and contraceptives themselves are practically unavailable. Adequate family-planning services should be provided to ensure the well-being and health of the whole family. State family-planning services should be created to ensure that information and medical assistance is provided to the entire population of reproductive age. Safe, modern forms of contraception should be made available. Public information and education programmes, including for young people, should be undertaken to ensure a full understanding of the set of family-planning measures available.

B. National mechanisms for the affairs of women, their structure, functions and role in *perestroika* processes*

The advancement of women in any country is inseparably linked to the tasks and specific aspects of its own development. Therefore different priorities may be identified at different stages. None the less east European countries have many common political and economic relationships that have affected the social status and social awareness of women during the transition to a market oriented economy. That transition has involved similar economic and political reforms in the USSR as well as in eastern Europe

_____

*   by Polina Maeva, Director, Department of Women's Affairs, Protection of the Family, Motherhood and the Child, USSR Cabinet of Ministers.

varying only in degrees of radicalism. A search for common strategies, tactical steps and comparative analysis of practical experience is essential.

The fundamental documents relating to the advancement of women that have been adopted by bodies and agencies of the United Nations, in particular the Convention on theElimination of All Forms of Discrimination against Women, played a positive role in women's issues in the 1980s, when a more favourable view with respect to the need for enhancing the status of women in the society as part of the global problem of human rights and development as a whole emerged.

Many acute problems were solved during the 1980s in the sphere of labour, daily life and protection of motherhood. The rates of maximum permissible loads for women during cargo handling operations were reduced, measures on special assistance to women in improving their professional skills were elaborated and specific comprehensive programmes for reducing manual labour in different industries were adopted. During that decade the USSR Government developed and strengthened the system of material assistance to families with children, which eventually ensured partial improvement of the lot of women in the family.

On numerous occasions the size of allowances to single mothers, wives of soldiers on regular military service and disabled children were reviewed and increased. Numerous new allowances were introduced that established preferential allocation of housing to single mothers, mothers of twins and families with many children, granted the right to receive easy-term credits for young families and introduced free medicines for children under three years of age and free distribution of baby food for children under two years of age from low-income families and families with many children.

Bearing in mind the high involvement of women in social production, a policy was introduced to develop and organize public catering, trade and other services at their place of work. According to statistical data various domestic services were provided directly at the place of work to 80 per cent of women, trade services to 70 per cent , cultural services to 60 per cent, physical culture and sports services to 86 per cent and public catering to 30 per cent.

The State supported the desire of women to obtain higher and secondary education by providing various kinds of assistance.

Fundamental issues relating to the improvement of the conditions of work, household life and self-fulfilment of women have not yet been solved.

With a view to alleviating the problems existing in the services sphere, the Government has undertaken a major economic step that is basically aimed at redistributing material and financial resources towards the sphere of social services (education, public health, culture) that has increasingly attracted consumer interest and, to a large extent, determined the prospects for active social involvement of an individual. That step has been well justified. The period 1986-1990 saw higher rates of construction compared with 1981-1985. The results of that measure were a lower divorce rate (from 3.5 per 1,000 population to 3.3), a lower rate of infant mortality and lower maternal mortality.

Fifty-eight per cent of children attended pre-school establishments. The crime rate among women decreased by 16 per cent in 1988 compared with 1984.

Undoubtedly those were important measures and their social results are no less important, however, they have a local nature. They have not helped to radically change either the status of women or the status of the family. One of the main causes - level of economic development - remained and consequently there exists the need for low-skilled women's labour. In politics production interests still prevail over social ones.

Scientific and technological progress is aimed primarily at achieving production targets and ignores the need to improve working conditions. The organizational and technological levels of production make it impossible to ensure the development of women's skills and to introduce alternative working regimes more convenient for women despite the Government's declarations that it would relieve women from hard manual jobs.

The great intellectual potential of women engaged in industry is not fully used. In spite of the fact that women account for 60 per cent of engineers, 87 per cent of economists and accountants, 40 per cent of scientific workers, and two thirds of medical workers, the number of women among heads of enterprises and organizations has decreased and, in 1985, women accounted for only 6.9 per cent of people holding such positions. That limited their opportunities for participating at all levels of administration and management.

All those factors taken together hamper women's development, adversely affect families and make the task of creating new technological structures in industrial production almost unattainable. Women's transfer from harmful and hard jobs to the service sector is also difficult to attain without a dramatic change in the system of remuneration in non-productive branches. As experience has shown, women would risk their health rather than agree to a lower paid job.

However, renovation of society, which has already begun, its movement towards such fundamental objectives as democratization, harmonization of relations within the society, recognition of individual's interests, qualitative replacement of existing productive forces, creation of a new technological structure, economic freedom of citizens and introduction of better incentives, greater labour and economic activity, self-management responsibility of each person for his or her well-being, enhanced role for the individual in society's development, which are essential for reaching those goals, clearly demonstrate that the ongoing process of renovation will be greatly hampered if the position of women in economy, society and the family is not changed.

The late 1980s saw the first alarming signs that a considerable portion of working women could actually become victims of *perestroika* due to their poor professional training and numerous social benefits during the period of transition to a market economy.

In the economy, the process of the establishment of cooperatives, joint-stock companies, joint ventures and leasing relations revealed that women seemed to be an unwelcome asset from an economic viewpoint.

In politics, women lost in the fierce competition during the elections which for the first time were held on an alternative basis. During the 1989 elections to the Supreme Soviet the number of women deputies decreased by half from 33 to 15.5 per cent. The results of the elections in the republic and local Soviets were even worse. For instance, only 5.3 per cent of women were elected to the Supreme Soviet of the Russian Federation, 2.9 per cent to the Supreme Soviet of the Ukrainian SSR and 3 per cent to the Supreme Soviet of the Byelorussian SSR.

In the social sphere, women have been the first to feel the consequences of the unbalanced consumer market, aggravated inter-ethnic problems, forced migration from some republics and complications in inter-ethnic marriages. Growing confrontation of political forces in the country has created a threat that women could become victims of political manipulations and time-serving approaches in solving employment problems. It has become evident that conservative patriarchal views of woman's place in society are becoming increasingly popular in the press, where only women's maternal function is elevated. Eighty per cent of women responding to questions in a recent sociological poll categorically objected to confining their life to the maternal role alone.

Women feel a need to institutionalize their activities. New women's movements, organizations and associations are springing up. They have never been as diverse in terms of the content of their activities, their objectives, their territory and nationality.

In short, the problem of true equality between men and women, employment of women as well as the quality of the women's workforce has become acute. As diverse forms of ownership begin to emerge it has become necessary to define new parameters of social protection for women and families. It has become apparent that society has to deal with "women's issues" at the level of State policy. That need was voiced by the first Congress of the USSR peoples deputies at the end of 1989. It entrusted the Government with the task of elaborating a long-term comprehensive programme for the advancement of women that included issues of labour conditions, daily-life problems as well as the question of mother-and-child protection.

That programme was to define the objectives, principles, guidelines and priorities of a single policy for the advancement of women, social support of the family and mother-and-child health-care. The programme was also to elaborate a course of action for all levels of administration and all forms of ownership aimed at the general improvement in the quality of life, particularly of that of women and families.

The programme was also to formulate measures aimed at solving the problems that had emerged in the areas of professional employment of women, family life and rearing of children that had led to the erosion of basic structures of society, deterioration of conditions for reproduction of the population and decreased efficiency of public production and labour potential of the country.

The programme was to assist the transfer to a market economy and to counter destabilizing processes in society, to secure the vital interests of women and families in the framework of the activity of the USSR Government, the governments of republics as well as local governing bodies. In solving the existing problems and crisis situations those governments should not lose sight of a comprehensive strategy for the advancement of women and families in society.

In view of the fact that the sovereignty of republics is expanding and 75 million people or every fourth Soviet citizen (including a significant number of women) currently live outside their republics, the programme had to contain a new system of social protection of women, families and children irrespective of the region of their current residence.

That complex task required objective reliable statistics, scientific research and forecasts, use of international expertise, a profound analysis of the status of women in the area of labour and family, and consolidated of efforts all ministries, agencies, economic bodies, public organizations and movements as well as scientists.

In solving that problem the need was felt to

transform specialized State institutions into a national mechanism to deal with the problems of women and families.

This mechanism consists of a standing committee on women's affairs, family protection and demography within the framework of the USSR Supreme Soviet. A department on women's affairs, mother, child and family protection has also been set up within the framework of the USSR Cabinet of Ministers.

A Directorate with a similar name has been established within the framework of the USSR State Committee on Labour and Social Issues.

The main functions of a Committee of the Supreme Soviet are law-making and supervision.

In its support a department within the USSR Cabinet of Ministers has been entrusted with analytical, expert, coordination and organizational function in the changing situation of women. It works on possible ways and methods of solving problems and then presents its conclusions to the USSR Government. It also examines and summarizes the legal practice in the area of family policies and social aid to women and children in the Soviet republics and abroad. It organizes the elaboration and supervises the implementation of specific decisions taken by the USSR Supreme Soviet and the Cabinet of Ministers. It assesses all draft laws and decisions in terms of safeguarding the interests of women, families and children. It initiates the discussion of women and family issues at the collegiums of the USSR ministries. It organizes training of decision-making administrative officers and influences public awareness regarding the need for improving the status of women.

The functions of the Directorate of the USSR State Committee on Labour are to elaborate the guidelines for the advancement of working women, family policies, draft laws and decisions, specific programmes and regulations as well as to build the system of social protection of workers with families.

The fundamental problems that have been solved over the short period of 18 months by the structures of the USSR national mechanisms are given below.

The efforts of scientists dealing with women's problems in the USSR have been consolidated, their research activities have been appropriately directed which has helped in the elaboration, with the participation of the USSR Academy of Sciences, of a concept of the State policy for the advancement of women and families as well as mother-and-child protection.

More than 30 USSR ministries, agencies, and academic and public organizations prepared for the first time in the history of the country "Fundamentals of State Policy for the Advancement of Women, the Family, Mother-and Child-Protection: Programme of Action for the 1990s".

The drafting of special-purpose programmes for the advancement of women has been initiated in many republics coupled with a nation-wide baby-food production programme.

Many legislative acts relating to women and the family have been reviewed and given expert assessment; legal regulations are being revised and brought into line with new social and economic conditions.

Among the important achievements is the development of a new system of benefits payable to families with children, and compensation to offset rising prices.

It is important to note that the Committee for Women, the Family and Demographic Policies of the USSR Supreme Soviet held hearings on the implementation of the Convention.

A specially designed training course entitled "Status of women in modern society: family policies. Social dimensions of mother and child care" is being used to educate parliamentarians, administrators, managerial and economic personnel.

Although the advancement of women is a lengthy and slowly developing process, it is hoped that better knowledge and a realization of the importance of resolving women's problems for development prospects will shape new attitudes and help to intensify efforts.

All the structures of the national mechanism are working together to ensure the functioning of a multi-channel system of information and consultative assistance for women and families receiving government social assistance on questions concerning their allowances, benefits and social guarantees. These are also responsible for developing different forms for exchanging information with international organizations.

The functioning of the nation-wide mechanism serves as an incentive for setting up similar bodies in union republics. But for each of these republics, the advancement of women can take on quite a different meaning given specific regional differences in women's issues. Hence the great diversity of republican structures involved with women's and family issues.

A Committee for Women, the Family and Demographic Policies has been set up under the Council of Ministers of the Russian Federation.

In the Cabinets of Ministers of Uzbekistan, Byelorussia, Kazakhstan and Tadjikistan departments have been created to resolve the problems of women, the family, mother-and-child care. Some republics have set up special divisions to tackle these problems. In the Ukraine, Estonia and Moldova, consultants have been appointed to study issues regarding the family and the status of women.

Special structures are being created in numerous executive committees of district Soviets of People's Deputies, with the USSR and Uzbekistan leading the process.

A number of ministries and enterprises have created special services, offices or commissioners to implement the policy of the advancement of women and the family.

The Institute for Socio-Economic Studies on Population under the USSR Academy of Science and the State Labour Committee of the USSR have set up a Centre for Gender Studies.

As mentioned earlier, all the structures of the national mechanism are geared to develop the most important strategic document called "Fundamentals of State Policy for the Advancement of Women, the Family, Mother-and Child-Protection: Programme of Action for the 1990s".

The Programme of Action for the 1990s was presented as an inalienable part of the social policy of the State and of the economic reform. The policy laid down in that document was indicative in nature and was called upon to serve as a scientific and methodological basis for developing special-purpose regional, republican, local and industrial (branch) programmes that would take into account economic, social, demographic, ethnic and other particular conditions in each of the territories, industries and branches. At the same time minimal and mandatory social guarantees would be set at the national level to cover all the population.

The document consisted of three sections: advancement of women in the sphere of labour; family policies; mother-and-child care.

The Programme of Action serves as a methodological basis for resolving women's and family issues within a wider framework of social programmes that include labour, housing and retirement legislation, demographic policy and social security. They correspond with the Universal Declaration of Human Rights, the Declaration of Social Progress and Development, the Convention on the Elimination of All Forms of Discrimination against Women and other international instruments. They include informational and scientific substantiation of the programme, implementation machinery, financial implications and expected social results, as well as background information that helps to identify the nature, depth and regional specificity of problems, to determine the necessary orientation of the republican programmes with due regard to local conditions, material basis and the level of development of public movements and initiatives supporting women and families.

State policy for the advancement of women in the sphere of employment was based on the recognition of the fact that women were an active force in the period of transformation and that their employment and motherhood were of equal social significance. The measures to be implemented are not limited to traditional and inefficient practices of increasing benefits and privileges for hazardous working conditions, instead they are aimed at improving the working conditions of all workers through scientific and technological progress and the elimination of jobs that threaten working women's maternal health; improve their skills and competitiveness; mobility of women in the employment market, their training for socially prestigious jobs, employment diversification, changing employment schedules. In implementing those measures preference would be given to economic incentives.

In order to implement those measures the State has assumed responsibility for job training and re-training, which is reflected in the "Fundamentals of the USSR and Republican Employment Legislation" as well as in the draft law "On Vocational Training in the USSR". Working women with young or handicapped children would be given most favoured treatment. After or during child-care leave they may undergo professional rehabilitation. At the national, republican and local levels State employment agencies are being established to prevent discrimination and to ensure equal job opportunities. For that purpose the functioning of similar agencies in France, Germany and Sweden have been studied in some detail.

State agencies are called upon to achieve a balance between the professional and family roles of women, to promote their entrepreneurial efforts and to facilitate their participation in political and social decision-making at all levels.

State family policy is based on the assumptions that the well-being of families is contingent upon the labour contribution of their members, and that the State should provide greater support to families and their disabled members in times of hardship; that the family has freedom of choice of the form of its economic support; that a social partnership of State bodies and of public, religious and charity organizations would improve the conditions and standard of living of families; that nation-wide and regional measures should be combined with account taken of the specificity of the socio-economic and demographic development of various territories.

The programme of action has singled out as a priority, policies regarding the family; the establishment of a new system of economic support for families objectively needing such assistance; creation of propitious conditions for combining parenthood with gainful employment; and enhanced psychological and pedagogical assistance to families.

The mechanisms of implementation have been envisaged as the following:

(a) Tax rebates for certain types of family, credits, loans;

(b) Legal and economic support for family enterprises;

(c) Preferential social guarantees regarding employment for members of large families, one-parent families and other objectively needy families;

(d) Direct financial assistance to families with children in time of acute need and indexation of fixed allowances;

(e) Transfer of subsidies from the sphere of production to the sphere of consumption;

(f) Consultative assistance to families with problems;

(g) Extension to fathers and other family members of benefits and privileges that were previously granted only to mothers.

The State policy of health-care for mothers and children has identified as a top priority measures aimed at solving problems that affect the genetic fund and the health of the nation, the provision of medico-genetic assistance to the population, prophylaxis of innate defects and diseases, the development of specialized medical assistance services for women and children, and satisfying the demand for special food compounds for infants. These priorities will to a large extent determine the health of the country's population and thus will also determine the degree of success in the social and economic development of society both in the immediate future and the long term.

The position paper was discussed and approved by the Cabinet of Ministers of the USSR and is now being examined in the USSR Supreme Soviet, while work to ensure its implementation has already begun. A whole range of interrelated measures is being taken:

(a) The legal basis for entrepreneurship has been worked out;

(b) A draft law "On the Protection of Labour in the USSR" has been elaborated taking into account the decrease in the volume of direct State controls over labour conditions;

(c) Bearing in mind that economic dependence is the basis for all other forms of dependence, steps are being taken to eliminate the substantial differences in salaries in the various branches of the economy despite the difficult financial situation of the country. A new system of labour remuneration is being introduced in sectors not directly involved in production, which employ mainly women. The scale of basic salaries and wages here is increased by 1.7-1.8 times and will practically eliminate the gap in labour remuneration with workers directly involved in the production sphere;

(d) A reliable system of employment insurance and social support of the population meeting the conditions of a market economy is being established. Pensions and scholarships for students have been increased and the system of support for families with children has been reoriented in accordance with the pattern that was long ago tried and tested in many countries of the world. Monthly allowances to single mothers until their children reach the age of 16-18 have been added to pregnancy and childbirth allowances and allowances for the new-born and care during infancy. The contingent of people eligible to receive those allowances has been broadened. The allowances will not be payable only to the most well-off families with a per capita income surpassing the equivalent of four minimal salaries. The amount of allowances has been raised to the level of a minimal salary. This principle is being consistently implemented throughout the whole system of social protection that is now being established in respect of pensions and scholarships providing for a possibility of their automatic indexation in case of inflation.

Compensatory payments have been introduced in connection with the increase in prices for manufactured goods and food products. This was done on a recipient-oriented basis in respect of every social group. Special compensation was envisaged in connection with the increase in prices for children's items. All this should ease, even if only partially, the situation of women with children. And as economic reform continues the system of social support for women, families and children should be consistently improved with its essential features corresponding to an ever greater degree to the patterns of a market economy.

C. Women and economic reform: State policy and social guarantees*

Introduction

Revision of State social policy has been an integral part of the process of reform in the USSR. The restructured socially-oriented market economy was based on a comprehensive system of economic, legal and social guarantees of the rights of every member of society, including the right to work and to an income that ensured an adequate standard and quality of life. State support, under such a system, would be provided to those who were incapable of securing an income sufficient to ensure this end. It was assumed those were most likely to be families with young parents, single-parent families, students, disabled persons, pensioners and others with a limited or reduced capacity to work.

The process of socio-economic restructuring in the USSR was aimed at improving every aspect of life within which the situation of women and families required particular attention. Women's employment, the functioning of the family and the rearing of children should all be examined and contradictions resolved to ensure that women's fundamental rights and those of the family and children were adequately represented at all levels of government and administration.

USSR Ministry of Labour and Social Affairs in the Structure of the National Mechanism to improve the situation of women, children and the family

In 1989, the First Congress of People's Deputies of the USSR adopted a resolution to develop a State programme to improve the situation of women including such issues as mother-and-child care. To that end, a national organization would be established that would deal specifically with those issues and others of concern to women. That national mechanism has taken shape in the past few years and includes the USSR Supreme Soviet Committee for the situation of women, protection of the family, mother-and-child care and departments in charge of the same issues within the USSR Cabinet of Ministers and the Ministry of Labour and Social Affairs. Similar organizations have also been established at republic and local levels.

The USSR Supreme Soviet Committee was in charge of drafting legislation and controlled the subsequent implementation. Legislation was developed in the context of international standards such as the Convention and other relevant documents of the United Nations and its specialized agencies. The Committee became a mechanism by which interdepartmental policy on women, children and the family was carried out. The relevant department of the USSR Cabinet of Ministers was an executive organ that ensured that the principle of equality, incorporated in the Constitution and various legislation, was applied. It also acted as a coordinating body for other relevant ministries and departments as well as for the republics of the USSR.

The Department for the status of women, protection of the family and mother-and-child care, established within the Ministry of Labour and Social Affairs, was responsible for the elaboration of an integrated, national social policy to safeguard women's rights in such areas as employment, social maintenance and working conditions and pay. The Department developed or took part in the development of draft laws and resolutions in the Congress of People's Deputies, the USSR Supreme Soviet and the Council of Ministers of the USSR. Moreover, it monitored the progress of implementation of the Convention, applications of laws, decrees and resolutions that concerned the situation of women, the family and mother-and-child care. Together with other organizations, the Ministry identified trends in women's employment and related issues and developed proposals to counter the problems identified. The Ministry also took part in the development and introduction of courses designed to upgrade the knowledge and skills of women workers so as to raise their professional and business status. Principles and mechanisms of social protection of women and families with children also fell within the scope of the activities of the Ministries.

The most important of the activities of the Departments was research, based on both Soviet and foreign experience, designed to determine conditions most favourable to the establishment of real equality between men and women and to the improvement of women's status in society. Under the jurisdiction of the Ministry, the Department coordinated the activities of other research institutions and, with the assistance of the Public Opinion Studies Centre, it organized sociological studies concerning women, the family, mothers and children. It also provided advice and assistance on women's issues to other federal ministries and departments, national trade-union committees and the Soviet Women's Committee.

---

* by Lyudmila Bezlepkina, Deputy Minister of Labour and Social Affairs.

Principles of State policy aimed at improving the situation of women, the family and children

The political, social and economic reforms in the USSR resulted in the development of a number of principles of policy to improve the situation of women, the family and mother-and-child care, rather than a national programme. The draft "Fundamentals of State Policy for the Advancement of Women, the Family, Mother-and Child-Protection: Programme of Action for the 1990s" was developed by the Ministry of Labour, on instructions from the USSR Government, in collaboration with many ministries, departments and research institutes and it incorporated proposals from the Soviet Women's Committee, the General Confederation of Trade Unions and other public organizations. The draft had been appraised and largely approved by a number of national and international experts including the Centre for Social Development and Humanitarian Affairs of the United Nations Office at Vienna.

In drafting the "Principles", a comprehensive approach was used for the first time. Social, economic, medical, ethnic and other factors relevant to the situation of women and children were taken into account. The "Principles" was, therefore, the first comprehensive document to define long-term State policy resting on the principles of a market economy aimed at improving the situation of women and the family and of mother-and-child care.

A single State policy with regard to women, children and the family was clearly needed for a number of reasons. Every republic of the USSR had its own economic, social, demographic and ethno-cultural features that required a specific approach to problem solving, and the existing economic links were inadequate for handling the problems associated with and arising from the changes that had occurred in the USSR. The fact that over 75 million people in the USSR lived outside their ethnic territories and 18 per cent of marriages were ethnically mixed contributed to the requirement for a national goal-oriented programme.

The programme of action was to be confined to the 1990s and embrace the most acute problems faced by women, including those concerning the labour status of women, choice between family and career, infrastructure of everyday life and support for families. The programme document was divided into three independent but interlinked sections: (a) principles of State policy to improve the situation of women; (b) principles of State policy regarding the family; and (c) principles of State policy in mother-and-child care. Further sections were devoted to the legal and organizational backing of the programme, information dissemination and financial backing.

The draft was supplemented by extensive reference material. The goals of the policy are summarized as follows:

(a) To ensure women's right to freely choose any socially useful occupation; and self-realization in work in the chosen trade, profession, studies, socio-political activities or rearing of children, or any combination of these;

(b) To ensure a higher status of the family in society and the creation of favourable conditions for its development; to ensure the right of the family to choose forms of economic, social and demographic behaviour that best suit them; and to enhance the role played by the family in the socialization of new generations;

(c) To create favourable conditions for bearing and rearing children.

Principles and trends of the State policy

The principles of the policy to improve the situation of women were based on the recognition of the active role played by women in the restructuring process, and the importance to society of women's labour and maternal functions. The main aims of the policy were to improve the social status of women, to promote equal opportunities for women to realize their interests and abilities in all spheres of public life, and to overcome existing inequality between men and women at work, in the family and in public and economic activity.

With regard to the family, the policy was based on the assumption that the family's well-being depended directly on the labour contribution of its members and the provision of State support in times of difficulty and to the disabled, but that the family was free to choose the method of economic support. Furthermore, cooperation between the State and non-governmental, religious and charity organizations was considered essential to effectively upgrade the situation of the family and a combination of national and regional measures should take into account the specific socio-economic and demographic features of the territories. Priority was given to the establishment of a new system of economic support for families, improving the infrastructure of everyday life and the provision of medical and psychological advice to families. In the area of mother-and-child care, priority was given to resolving the health problems associated with maternity and childhood including the development of specialized medical services and the provision of special food for young children. It was believed that the results of such measures would largely determine the socio-economic situation of society in the near and long term.

The initial implementation of the policy was largely due to its integration with the recently adopted more important social laws and measures. The Fundamental Legislation of the USSR and constituent republics of the USSR on employment, drafted by the Ministry of Labour and Social Issues and adopted by the Supreme Soviet in January 1991, was one such law designed to ensure the full and effective employment of all citizens. The law sets minimum levels of social protection in the event of unemployment and preserves the priority role of the State in the provision of equal opportunities for employment as well as in the prevention of unemployment. Additional employment guarantees, such as specialized enterprises and special training programmes, were provided to particular sections of the population considered more at risk, such as the young, single parents and disabled persons. The Legislation also provided for the development of similar State programmes. The practical implementation of the policy was the responsibility of the State employment service in which special posts had been established to provide occupational advice and guidance to women. Efforts were also made to create additional opportunities for women to enhance their competitiveness in the employment market. Broadening employment alternatives, including the development of small businesses, as well as providing vocational training and retraining and education were a few of the measures designed to ensure employment of women in the new situation.

A further resolution "On the Reform of Retail Prices and Social Protection of the Population", adopted by the USSR Cabinet of Ministers on 19 March 1991, aimed at preserving the living standards of families with children based on a system of allowances. With the reform of retail prices these allowances increased on average by 60-80 per cent. Allowances to parents of children under 16 years of age and to parents of students under 18 and receiving no scholarship were introduced. In addition, all families with children under 18 years were entitled to an annual allowance, the amount dependent upon the age of the child, as subsidies on goods have been discontinued.

A significant move towards implementing the policy to improve the situation of women, the family and children, was the passing of two related resolutions, the first, passed on 10 April 1990, "On Adequate Measures to Improve the Situation of Women, and Ensure Adequate Mother and Child Care and a Stronger Family" and the second, passed on 2 August 1990, "On Additional Measures in Social Protection of Families with Children in the Situation of Transition to a Regulated Market Economy. As much as 13 billion roubles had been allocated for the implementation of measures provided for in those resolutions.

XIII. YUGOSLAVIA

A. Women and the new democracy*

Perhaps the period since the changes began in eastern Europe and Yugoslavia has been too short for the effects of the restructuring to be adequately assessed but it has been long enough to be able to identify a number of trends, particularly with regard to the situation of women. At the beginning of restructuring, women were on the streets demonstrating, they were holding meetings, waving flags and banners, shouting, singing and voting. But when it came to forming new governments, when it came to direct participation in power, women became invisible again. The new democratic arrangements were supposed to improve the situation of everyone - men and women - yet women are in real danger of losing many of the rights they had previously been granted.

Bearing in mind the diverse cultural, historical and geographical situation of the Yugoslav people as well as the large differences that exist between the republics in employment, natality and standard of living, it is difficult to speak of the "Yugoslav woman". The changes that have occurred, the declarations of independence, elections and constitutional changes, have resulted in an extremely complex political situation that further complicates discussion of the situation of Yugoslavian women. The country has increasingly divided along a number of issues, most importantly as to whether Yugoslavia should become a centralized federal State or a decentralized, loose confederation. Rising nationalism, fear of civil war and a deepening economic crisis has obfuscated analysis of the situation of women. Furthermore, as demographic data have been drawn from the 1981 Census and no new research is available, trends could only be identified in the responses of new governments to women.

The percentage of women participating in formal decision-making processes is a major indicator of the status of women. During the past 45 years, on average, 30 per cent of representatives in the parliaments were women. That was both usual and obligatory. After the recent elections women's representation in the parliaments of the republics fell to between 5 and 10 per cent. Previously, women's participation was token and they often had no real power and were unable to influence or effect policy. The drop in the level of representation of women could reflect (a) real interest of women in politics; and (b) real interest of the electoral body in voting for women. The low level of representation of women in politics also reflects both the existing political culture and patriarchal

social arrangements. But it may not be a temporary phenomenon.

The strong influence of the Croatian Democratic Union (HDZ) and other conservative nationalist parties, particularly in Croatia and Slovenia, gave rise to a more traditional image of women. Prior to the elections, that image was used and promoted in policy statements made to voters and undoubtedly influenced their voting behaviour. Subsidies, for example, were promised to women who had three or more children, while concern was expressed about overworked women and that consideration should be given to them to fulfil their primary and "sacred" duty of homemaking. Women were to be confined to the roles of child-bearer and housewife. The role allocated to women was reflected in the election results in Slovenia and Croatia: the former has one woman minister and the latter none; 10 per cent of the representatives in the Croatian Parliament are women and only 4.8 per cent in the Slovenian Parliament. Given that situation, to what extent would women be able to influence policy and to defend the rights of 53 per cent of the population?

The status of women is also reflected in the drafts of the new constitutions. Three republics have not so far altered their constitutions and a fourth, Serbia, has, but without adversely affecting women. Although a number of changes have been proposed concerning taxes and abortion rights, they have not been passed largely due to strong lobbying from Serbian women's groups. However, the Slovenian (under discussion) and Croatian (passed December 1990) draft constitutions are both of some concern. Difficulties arose with the first sentence of the Slovenian draft ("The Constitution originates from the sanctity of life.") which the Minister of Culture explained directly referred to the prohibition of abortion. Furthermore, the language in the Constitution was of the masculine gender and often ambiguous, and when women were referred to in two articles of the draft it was only as mothers, that is, as persons under the special protection of the Republic. Articles 52 and 45 have caused particular concern to women as they sought to limit their right to freely decide on maternity and access to abortion. A number of women's groups have proposed amendments to these articles and although those are still being discussed many women are concerned that the new Constitution would form the foundation to a strong pro-life abortion law. The draft Constitution of the Republic of Croatia is still more conservative,

---

*   by Slavenka Drakulic.

based on often arbitrary criteria, such as public morals, often contradictory, and it effectively limits the rights of all citizens but more particularly those of women. Although one draft article promoting the right to life of every unborn child was eventually dropped from the Constitution after protests from women's organizations, implicit in a number of others is an increased role for women as carers. Both draft constitutions only recognize a maternal function for women that ultimately seeks to limit their advancement.

Although the pro-life stance of the conservative parties has been clearly stated and has been incorporated into party platforms, it is not a serious issue for public discussion. Unfortunately, because the real issue at stake appears to be democracy itself, the pro-life agenda has been largely ignored in the election process. Women are no exception. Comprising 53 per cent of the population, many women must have voted for the HDZ programme (gender-disaggregated statistics on voting patterns are unavailable) and thus potentially for restricted access to abortion. Potentially in the sense that such a law has not been passed but all indications suggest that it was on the political agenda particularly given the current low birth rate in Croatia. Women have on average 1.8 children and many people fear that Croatia will "disappear". Although the Croatian Government has not articulated a population policy, the strong ties between the new Government and the Catholic Church as well as other indications, such as the showing of the baptism of every eleventh child on television, have rendered that policy direction reasonably clear. The situation is very similar in Slovenia and in Serbia.

The minimal involvement of women in political life in the republics is only one indication of their general status. Economic conditions, especially arising from employment conditions, would have a greater immediate effect on women. According to previous research, the average income of women is between 20 and 40 per cent lower than that of men, women are less educated than men, and they are concentrated at the lower levels of the occupational hierarchy, in particular in such industries as textiles, and in the social services. Again, the situation of women varies from republic to republic, according to the level of development, but the current economic crisis has exacerbated existing problems and has led to a fall in industrial production and a dramatic increase in the numbers of persons unemployed. The majority of the unemployed are women. The growing poverty in Yugoslavia will contribute to an increase in the number of women dismissed from employment precisely because of where they work, and traditional values will be reasserted and women will be discouraged from seeking new employment. A patriarchal mentality will probably prevail even though it is extremely difficult for a family to exist on one wage.

Equality cannot be achieved without a strong economic base.

The mass media also plays a role in shaping the situation of women in society. Although the political changes during 1989-1990 brought changes in the media, those changes did not follow the expected course. Legal changes meant that new newspapers could be established but those proved neither independent nor objective. Media that had formerly been centrally controlled or subject to "autocensorship" came under the influence of the ruling political parties. Although those organs were financially independent, the top executives of television and radio stations in Slovenia and Croatia were appointed and controlled by the Government. In that environment women's issues could be effectively manipulated. Women were portrayed in their roles as mothers and homemakers, their economic function was ignored. The difficulties of single mothers, the level of unemployment among women and their poor remuneration were not discussed. The feminization of poverty and sexism were not considered interesting. One illustration of the role the media played in forming public opinion about women and women's roles was the degree and type of publicity that was given to the opening of Croatia's first brothel: "The public, irritated by streetwalkers, can finally rest - there is now a brothel open in Zagreb, tailored to suit gentlemen." The article suggested that women and their emancipation were to blame for that situation. Similarly, the dramatic increase in the number of sex shops and pornographic magazines for sale was touted, by the media, as indicative of a move towards the great way of life of the West.

Virtually nobody was in a position to confront that blatant manipulation of women. The media itself was at worst government controlled and at best inherently conservative; the opposition both within and outside of parliament was weak; and women's organizations were small and lacking in financial or institutional assistance. Women themselves were confused by the new situation and the growing nationalist feeling effectively prohibited any activity that could have appeared anti-government. All of which begged the question, what now? The answer was not easy particularly as the feeling among many women was "let us go home and have some rest". Many felt that they had been forcibly emancipated and that emancipation meant a dirty, heavy, boring job followed by many more hours working in the home. True emancipation probably existed only on paper and in reality women were subordinated to men in every sphere of life.

Women's organizations were also problematic for many women due to the legacy of the communist regime. The Yugoslav Communist Party, the leading organization of resistance and revolution from 1941 onwards, mobilized and organized some 2 million women into the Antifascist Women's Front (AWF), and of them more than 100,000 fought in the partisan forces. Although many women were killed or injured, women found liberation in the War because they were treated as equal to men. For the first time in their lives they were not viewed as sex objects or household property. Soon after the War, AWF became the bureaucratic women's organization that served to assure the maintenance of Communist Party power over women. Other independent women's organizations were forbidden as efficient control required institutionalization. The end of the 1970s saw the advent of a new generation of women who were prepared to challenge the official view of the status of women and the gap between Marxist theory and social processes. Thus the first public articulation of feminist thinking occurred in 1978 at a non-governmental international conference on women, held at Belgrade, to which feminists from France, the Federal Republic of Germany, Hungary, Italy, Poland and the United Kingdom of Great Britain and Northern Ireland had been invited. The media claimed that as a declaration of war between the sexes and it was also a matter of contention between women as the women war veterans viewed feminism as synonymous with disloyalty to Yugoslavia. But some women persevered, and by the end of 1979 approximately 30 of them had formed the group "Women and Society". They wrote articles, promoted public discussion and held lectures on previously unquestioned issues. In the 10 years or so since then, many new and different groups have formed but to date no mass involvement of women in that movement has been seen.

The problems of women, both recent and inherited, can only be solved when women organize themselves. Unfortunately, a number of obstacles must be overcome to achieve that aim. The concept of feminism itself has been abused by the media and reduced to women who hate men, and as a result very few women would publicly identify themselves as feminist. Women baulk at the idea of organizing as reminiscent of the official and so distrusted women's organizations. Women also have to learn to take responsibility for their position into their own hands and not entrust it to the Government. To abrogate responsibility now to the Government would be disastrous for women, as outlined above. Women should also learn that the degree to which they have rights equal to those of men to access and opportunity will be the degree to which democracy may be said to be functioning effectively in society, and democracy as it was in Yugoslavia defined emancipation in male terms only. If women do not defend their rights and claim an adequate role in political decisions, they should accept some responsibility for their situation.

Future research on the situation of women in Yugoslavia should be conducted in every republic and should focus on the following key areas:

(a) Changes in legislation after elections, if any;

(b) Women's participation in political life;

(c) Unemployment of women and loss of social benefits;

(d) The image of women in the media;

(e) The influence of nationalism, population policy and political use of women.

B. The impact of reforms on the status of women*

Introduction

The system that until recently existed in Yugoslavia guaranteed many rights to women and a variety of services to the family. Among those, the most important was constitutionally guaranteed equality between the sexes that also included freedom to decide on the number of children, guaranteed paid maternity leave, paid leave for one parent in case of the illness of a child, medical care and related services to women in connection with pregnancy, childbirth and family planning, safety at work, children's allowance and pre-school and school-child care. The status of women varied considerably, however, between the various republics and between regions within the republics and was dependent to a large degree on the level of development of those areas. Although many advances had been made in the status of women many problems remained.

The promotion of the status of women could be seen in the spheres of labour, education and maternity care. Women's share of the labour force increased from 24.2 per cent in 1954 to over 40 per cent in 1991 (46.7 per cent in Slovenia, the most developed republic). The rate of growth in women's employment in the post-war period was considerably higher than that of men. From the early 1980s, the beginning of the economic crisis, the rate of women's employment, together with overall employment, began to fall.

---

* by Vesna Pesic, Researcher, Department of Sociology, Institute of Social Sciences.

In spite of those achievements, women comprise the majority of those who are least well remunerated. Women also wait for work longer and tend to be oriented towards "female professions", largely due to an inadequate representation of female students at technical professional schools and faculties and over-representation in short-term educational institutions. Little change has occurred in traditional male and female roles,[1] women still undertake most of the household chores and their role within the family is clearly subordinate; violence against women is wide-spread and public awareness low, but is increasing due to the activities of feminist groups. The illiteracy rate for women is considerably higher than that for men. In 1981, 14.7 per cent of women compared with 4.1 per cent of men were illiterate. Women have had little influence on politics, reflected in the extremely low percentage of women in government agencies and women who have held high-level positions in enterprises.

Women's participation in formal education at all levels has increased. In 1985, 95 per cent of girls attended elementary education compared with 85 per cent in 1971. The number of girls who continue through secondary education also increased, although they currently comprise less than 50 per cent of students enrolled. A similar situation is observed at tertiary level. Women comprised 49.2 per cent of the total number of students enrolled in the 1989/90 academic year. No discrimination was made between men and women when granting scholarships and student credits.

Paid maternity leave is extended and guaranteed by federal law, although differences in the length of leave, from 180 to 365 days, exists between the republics. The financial position of women during maternity leave has also improved and the possibility for working shorter hours has increased.

The legal or de jure status of women in Yugoslavia is much more favourable than their de facto situation. One of the major reasons is that the concept of equality has been incorporated into the system as part of the communist ideology. The rights of women derive from the egalitarian values that underpinned the communist regime, but at the same time that such rights were granted, other rights, such as that to organize independently and publicly articulate their interests, were withdrawn or prohibited. Women are thus not prepared to deal with those changes and the growing conservative tendencies that have brought into question the exercise of their basic rights. On the one hand, women could lose the rights they have already acquired precisely due to the effects of economic and political reforms, while on the other hand, those very reforms create possibilities for women to free themselves from their "false emancipation" and artificial participation in politics. The new parties and elected authorities, however, show little interest in the problems and concerns of women. In the future therefore the struggle for women's rights will be dependent upon the independent organization of women and their participation in politics.

A number of negative consequences for the status of women could arise from the restructuring process. The established elements of equality between the sexes are under threat from rightist parties, of which some are overtly traditionalist and nationalist and see a woman's place as in the home bearing and rearing children. One expected effect of the economic reforms, which involves a transition to a market economy and the restructuring of the economy, has been a mass lay-off of waged labour. It has been assumed that women would be hardest hit in those lay-offs because "female professions" were considered more vulnerable than "male professions". The reforms are taking place in a situation marked by an almost complete financial collapse that could seriously affect the payment of maternity-leave allowances and other cash benefits, such as the children's allowance, free education and the availability of children's institutions and medical services. Finally, free political competition has led to a dramatic reduction in the number of women officials in government agencies and thus their influence on relevant and crucial political decisions has been effectively curtailed.

It was difficult to determine when reforms began - although 1989 was the year that the opposition parties were founded and multi-party elections were held in all republics - the direction they are taking and their effects. The process of change has been mediated by an increasing nationalism which has partly blocked economic reforms and multi-party elections at the federal level. The pace and direction of change has also differed between the republics, rendering discussion of "Yugoslav reform" difficult. However, in general the reforms have been directed towards eliminating inflation, developing a market economy and encouraging entrepreneurship, privatizing ownership and restructuring the economy. Each republic has followed its own programme, in which a ten-

---

[1] According to a study of the portrayal of women in history books used in elementary schools, "in spite of certain attempts to devote more attention to the historical role of women - in comparison to the previous generation - not much has been achieved in that respect. The results of the research show that history books are burdened with a masculine point of view...". See Rajka Poli, "The Masculine Point of View and the Animal Syndrome, Zena 48 (3-4) 11.30, Zagreb, 1990.

dency to preserve social ownership or introduce state ownership could be observed. Nevertheless, a large number of private firms, mainly small-scale businesses, have been established. Bearing that in mind, it is apparent that the effects these changes are having and will have on the status of women are difficult to determine. Tendencies, however, can be identified.

The disintegration of national mechanisms for monitoring and promoting the status of women

A number of factors could adversely affect the status of women in the period of transition or crisis, not least of which is the functioning of the federal agencies that control the monitoring and implementation of all ratified international conventions, including the Convention on the Elimination of All Forms of Discrimination against Women. The prevention of multi-party elections has inhibited the functioning of Yugoslav authorities and the Commission for monitoring the Convention at the federal level has effectively ceased to function. The republics have proclaimed themselves sovereign States and taken control of constitutional and legal regulations. They are not signatories to the Convention, however, and thus have no obligations to it. No government agency responsible for the status of women has been set up in the republics.2/ Proposals from independent women's organizations for the establishment of ministries or commissions to deal with women's issues have been rejected by the new governments in some of the republics. The new Serbian Parliament emphatically rejected the request made by the Belgrade Women's Lobby, the Women's Party and opposition deputies that a Ministry for Women should be set up. The same happened in Croatia. A number of "shadow governments", for example in Croatia and Slovenia, envisaged the establishment of governmental agencies for dealing with issues linked to the status of women. The newly elected authorities have largely ignored problems related to the status of women or concentrated only on the reproductive role of women, thus threatening the constitutional right to choose childbirth and, potentially, other women's rights.

Political changes also resulted in the abolishment of the Socialist Alliance of the Working People, the "official" socio-political organization within which conferences for the social status of women existed. Although a logical step in the process of eradicating the monopoly of the communist party and political organizations under its control, no organization has been developed to take over their activities for the promotion of the status of women. Independent

women's organizations began to organize but they have had almost no official support (with the exception of some opposition deputies and parties), and lack basic means to undertake this work, especially if their orientation is feminist. Such organizations are in the early stages of development and only existed in capital cities and some of the larger towns. Nevertheless, the work of those organizations is gaining momentum, covering such areas as violence against women, including protection of women, discrimination against women in political life, sexual repression and hidden discrimination in employment and lay-offs. Some women's organizations are linked to the church and pro-life campaigns and their activities are most extensive in Croatia, where the feminist trend is also the strongest. They tended to attract more funding and more understanding from authorities and conservative public opinion.

No national machinery has been created for dealing with immediate and long-term issues relating to the status and role of women in the socio-economic, political and cultural life of the country.

Legal equality

The Constitution was amended in 1988 but did not change the existing principle of equality between the sexes nor other rights that provided maternity and labour guarantees. As agreement has not been reached between the republics on the adoption of a new Constitution, however, in practice many such rights are no longer observed or have been removed. In the new Constitution of the Republic of Croatia, for example, the right to freely decide on the birth of children has been cancelled. However, the principle of equality of men and women before the law has been maintained.

Laws and other legal provisions pertaining to equality between the sexes in public, private and economic life has not been changed to the detriment of women. On the contrary, recent legislative changes have provided for the protection and promotion of the status of women equally in all the republics and provinces. Therefore, articles 2, 3 and 15 of the Convention are guaranteed.

Economic reforms and the status of women

The restructuring of the socialist economy to a market economy had an effect on the majority of the population. That period of transition was characterized by a fall in production, a fall in investments and

---

2/ In Slovenia, a government Commission for Women's Policy has been set up, composed of women deputies. However, that Commission's work is being hindered due to the lack of quorum.

personal incomes, a grave fiscal crisis and scarcity of capital, and a reduction in contributions for collective consumption due to the excessive taxation of enterprises. Restructuring of the economy and introduction of a new mode of enterprise organization and management were expected during that period. Those changes meant bankruptcy for a large number of enterprises that were no longer profitable, and the reorganization of many others. Massive economic and technological redundancies of the labour force were expected.

The economic status of women was threatened by such changes. Hidden discrimination against women in employment was intensified.[3] A disinclination to employ women in the new private enterprises and privatized social firms has not been observed. It could be expected that the reorganization of social and public services, with the consequent reduction of administrative staff, would most seriously affect women since they represent the majority of staff in such services. It is possible to speculate on what the future economic status of women in former socialist countries would be but the available data do not provide concrete indications.

Employment of women and the structure of employment

In 1987, Yugoslavia ratified ILO Convention No.156 on Equal Opportunities and Treatment of Male and Female Workers, Workers with Families and thus reaffirmed existing legislation. No changes were made to any regulations that guaranteed equality of access to and opportunity for employment.

The employment of women rose in the social sector throughout the period of reform. The employment of women in the social sector constantly increased in the period from 1954 to March 1990 and now exceeds 40 per cent. Between 1987 and 1990, during which period total employment in the social sector decreased, the share of women rose from 38.4 to 40.1 per cent. Although such increases were observed in all republics and provinces, women's share of employment was higher in the more developed regions of the country.

An examination of the structure of employment by sector, industrial branch and profession reveals no change in traditional "male" and "female" jobs. On the contrary, the concentration of women employed in traditional female activities, such as education and culture and social care, has intensified. That was also observed in the "female" sectors of industry, such as textile, leather, tobacco and printing, which are both labour-intensive and ill paid. Women were less likely to find employment in the better paid capital intensive industries. In March 1990, 75 per cent of workers in textile production were women compared with 69 per cent in 1973. In leather and fur processing and production of footwear and leather goods that share reached an average of 69 per cent (in the footwear industry, 92.4 per cent) compared with 59 per cent in 1973.

Lay-offs, unemployment and skills structure

The restructuring of the economy led to massive lay-offs of workers and large numbers of technologically redundant workers, although no reliable data exists as to the extent to which women are affected. Theoretically women and men have equal access to the protection guaranteed by law to workers affected by technological and economic restructuring although extra protection to workers with families could also be provided, but regulations governing that have been passed only in Macedonia and Croatia.

Large scale lay-offs, particularly in Croatia and Slovenia, began at the end of 1990. According to data supplied by the Employment Office of Croatia, there were 216,000 registered unemployed at the end of January 1991 in this republic, that is, 38 per cent more than in the same month a year earlier.[4] According to informal findings the reason was bankruptcy of a number of larger enterprises mainly employing men. Unemployment rates for men and women depended upon what enterprises went into liquidation, that is, whether they were traditionally "male" or "female". Indications are that lay-off regulations were violated, with workers on sick leave and women on maternity leave being fired, but that sexual discrimination (although it is not excluded) was not involved.

Measures aimed at improving the professional and skill levels of workers affected by the process of economic restructuring should be expanded and improved and made available equally to men and women. According to data available on lay-offs for 1988 and 1989 from the Federal Statistical Office, 49 per cent of women held professional qualifications, 50.6 per cent had been retrained and 46.9 per cent were undergoing training. It is uncertain whether that would be the case in the future.

---

[3] This is called "negative selection" in employment a phenomenon of favouring the male work-force due to the frequent absence of women from work (maternity leave, child illness etc.), fewer ambitions etc. See Katja Gatin "Discrimination against women in employment", Zena 48(3-4), pp. 59-72. Zagreb 1990.

[4] Data taken from the daily paper "Borba" of 18 February 1991.

It is evident that in spite of a high unemployment rate, 15 per cent, that the percentage of unemployed women is decreasing. Since 1983, the number of women seeking employment has decreased, although the absolute number of job seekers has increased. In 1987, women accounted for 55.8 per cent of unemployed persons, 54.2 per cent in 1989 and 53 per cent in 1990. Skilled and unskilled female workers find employment most easily, while the majority of unemployed women hold secondary and post-secondary school, including university, qualifications.

Education

The high unemployment rates among educated women can be explained by the vocational orientation of girls to the "female professions", which are less in demand. Although all types of school and levels of education are equally accessible for all people in Yugoslavia, options for "female schools" have not changed for decades. Of women who hold a secondary school economic diploma, 78 per cent are unemployed, as are 77 per cent of women graduates of secondary librarian schools, 86 per cent of nurses; 69.9 per cent of teachers and 83.7 per cent of social workers (post secondary). The same pattern applies to women with university education in the social and political sciences, pharmacy and architecture. Conversely, the unemployment rate for women mechanical engineers is only 14.3 per cent, and that of electrical engineers 23.3 per cent.

Income distribution

Equal compensation for equal work is guaranteed both by constitutional and statutory provisions. In practice, however, the average income of women is 10-20 per cent below the average income of men. That has been a long-standing problem that is caused by an uneven distribution of the female labour force and lower professional, educational and competitive features of the female population. The economic crisis, however, has further disadvantaged the material status of women and the family. General material insecurity has meant financial hardship for hundreds of thousands of workers, both men and women, who are often not assured of the minimum income. Social relief is also vulnerable to the economic crisis; scarce resources often mean that maternity benefits are not paid for months. Increased fees at kindergartens and crèches render them inaccessible to the lower income group and thus they have become an elitist urban privilege. In the past, only 2 per cent of rural children and 4 per cent of the children of single mothers were enrolled in these institutions. Increasingly difficult living conditions could have negative consequences for the status of women and ultimately slow its promotion.

Women and business

The participation of women in entrepreneurial activities is low, particularly in large business concerns. Women rarely occupy top level positions in enterprises or other organizations. In order to obtain a senior position or a promotion, a woman has to be much better than her male competitors. The higher the social standing of a position, in terms of reputation, income and power, the rarer it is to find a woman occupying it. Although that had been the rule for decades in Yugoslavia, indications had emerged that the new private firms had opened new possibilities for such entrepreneurial activity among women. Unfortunately, due to a lack of gender-disaggregated statistics of the ownership of private firms, that trend cannot be confirmed. However, approximately 100 women from private and social enterprises took part in an entrepreneurship training course organized by the Consulting Centre of the Federal Executive Council at Ljubljana. Considerable interest from women brought about the establishment of the Women Entrepreneurs Club that dealt with problems specific to women, such as coordinating family and business responsibilities. Furthermore, 38 per cent of the students enrolled at the recently founded School for Entrepreneurship Training at Ljubljana were women. The Independent Alliance of Women in Zagreb provided information on the procedure for registration and the opening of private firms. Such activity has not been initiated in other republics. Recently, a large number of shops, boutiques, and cafes and restaurants owned by women have been opened. Unfortunately, a number of businesses have also been opened by a man in his wife's name, which allows him both to keep his job in the social sector and to draw customers from there to his private firm.

Women and the decision-making process

The exceptionally small number of women who won seats in republican parliaments, 4.6 per cent compared to 19.1 per cent in the former one-party assemblies highlights the actual political status of women in Yugoslavia. Yet even under the one-party dictatorship system women did not play an important role in decision-making despite the fact that they were better represented in assemblies at all levels and in executive State bodies. Women entered one-party assemblies according to the parity principle, that did not apply to top-level party bodies, but occasionally their loyalty to the party enabled them to acquire an important position in the party or State bodies. The most important decision-making in communist regimes, however, was not made in parliaments, but in party bureaux, often by one person. The multi-party system exposed the political marginalization of women. Parliament has become a place where important decisions are made, which accounts for the poor representation of women. Of the more than 200 parties that existed in Yugoslavia, only one had a woman president (if the few female parties and the green party are excluded).

The 1990 election results showed that women in Slovenia fared best, accounting for 11.3 per cent of elected deputies, and in Serbia the worst with only 1.6 per cent.[5] The percentage of women elected to parliaments in Croatia was 4.44, in Montenegro 4, in Macedonia 3.33 and in Bosnia-Herzegovina 2.92. The assertion that women were discriminated against in political processes in Yugoslavia was further supported by the low percentage of women nominated as candidates. In Bosnia-Herzegovina, for example, of 1,525 candidates only 85, or 5.57 per cent, were women. In Slovenia, 18.47 per cent of candidates nominated were women, but in Serbia only 4.98 per cent were women.

Research conducted on women in political parties showed that their involvement was much higher than to the number of female nominees in political parties.[6] It was also important that women candidates usually contested electoral units that parties did not expect to win. Moreover, women were placed at the end of election lists in those republics in which the proportionate electoral system applied. Women were also more often nominated by left and liberal parties, as in Slovenia and Croatia, or by smaller parties and those with minimal expectation of electoral success. Of the 246 candidates nominated by the Socialist Party of Serbia, the largest party, only 7 were women; the Democratic Party nominated 10 women of 183 candidates; while the Green Party nominated 9 women out of a total of 33 candidates. Women were also poorly represented on Steering Committees, formed after the elections. Of 27 ministers in Slovenia, only 2 were women, and in Serbia, of 20 candidates only 1 was a woman. In republics that have presidencies, that is a collective head of State, women were represented as follows: Bosnia-Herzegovina - 1 woman; Montenegro - 1 woman; Slovenia - none. Finally, the "reform" federal Government, which was formed in 1989, did not have a single female minister.

The free competition for power in the Yugoslav republics has resulted in the marginalization of women. The conviction prevails that women are politically less competitive and female candidates are destined to fail. Such conclusions accord with the traditional and patriarchal attitudes that have resurfaced in the current atmosphere of nationalistic fervour. Those attitudes and atmosphere had banished women from State bodies. The fact that women did not fare better in elections in other former socialist countries, nor in the recent elections for Western-European parliaments indicates that the participation of women in decision-making merits careful study with a view to elaborating adequate strategies for improvement.

Changes in the role of women and men in society and family

Legally, discrimination against women in marriage, divorce and family relations does not exist. None the less, family relations belonged to that sphere of life in which there is the greatest difference between de jure and the de facto status of women. All available research on the division of housework and family obligations and on the distribution of authority within the family, demonstrates that it is women who bear the bulk of the burden related to housework and child-rearing but that it is the husband who makes the final decisions.[7] Democratic decision-making and a more equal division of family duties, primarily those involving children and to a lesser extent housework, exist between husbands and wives of younger and better educated couples. More often among this group, husbands took leave when children were ill. In lower socio-economic groups the woman's position has become increasingly difficult, and it is worst within peasant families.

Violence against women in the family, not publicly discussed until fairly recently, is a major problem. It has been established that every 15 minutes a woman is beaten or molested (in 80 per cent of cases by her husband, former husband or common law husband). An independent women's organization started an SOS telephone line for women and children who are victims of violence, under the slogan "Let us make the violence visible". One in four women who called the SOS line complained that she had been threatened with murder, while 1 in 10 complained of being sexually molested by her partner. More than half of the women stated that the violence occurred daily while 75 per cent claimed that it had gone on for several years.[8]

---

[5] The truly "male parliament" in Serbia incited independent organizations of women to initiate the formation of a "female parliament" to deal with all issues of interest to women. This parliament was formed on 8 March 1991.

[6] See Smiljana Leinert Novosel, Women - a Political Minority, Zagreb, 1990.

[7] Andjelka Milic and Vesna Pesic, Family and Society, Belgrade 1982. A more recent study, which compared politically active and non-active women in terms of their housework duties has shown that both groups of women do all the housework alone in more than 50 per cent of cases. Smiljana Leinert Novosel, op. cit., p. 1 0 1.

[8] Data by the Belgrade SOS Line.

The social role of women has come under strong pressure from the neo-conservative authorities in almost all east European countries, including the Yugoslav republics. An indication of a clear bias exists against equality and the activity of pro-feminist women's organizations. In many parts of Yugoslavia, the traditional female model has been publicly promoted, which often includes the following: "Woman is the mother of the nation" and therefore her most important role is the reproductive one; "Woman is the heart of the family", whereby she is being pushed out of the social and economic development. That type of propaganda also has practical consequences as given below.

The first provision of the new Act on the Social Protection of Children read: "Social protection of children is an organized social activity which ensures realization of the policy of population renewal as well as provision of aid to the family in the achievement of its reproductive function...". The social and protective functions of this system were secondary, its primary function was reproductive. This is illustrated by the nature of the provision of financial aid for children of poor families: "Financial aid shall be extended to the family in order to stimulate population renewal. ... Those families which lack appropriate material conditions for child-care ... shall be entitled to financial aid for the first and the second child. Families with three children shall be entitled to financial aid for the third child regardless of material conditions". The Croatian Programme of Economic Policy for 1991 promises a right to retirement to parents with three or more children, while financial aid is to be given to all families.2/ It does not comply with article 11 (c) of the Convention.

Resolutions on population policy and family planning (federally and in some republics) subordinated the individual right to make decisions on child bearing to the general population policy goals and to increased fertility. Although they have no binding force in law, those new drafts of family planning laws were aimed at the curtailment of that individual right. More frequent references, mostly in Croatia and Slovenia, are made to the "sanctity of life", thus threatening the right to abortion. Signs also exist of attempts to make divorce more difficult and to re-

move equal treatment of legal and common-law marriages.

Development policy programmes in various republics envisage a reduction in women's employment. That is to be achieved by a reduction of approximately 20 per cent in the work-force in the feminized spheres of work, in education, health and child-care. In Slovenia, it is planned to employ out-of-work men on public works, while unemployed women are to be streamlined into working with the aged, the sick and the handicapped.

Finally, the centralization that is under way in all Republics has drastically reduced the independence of local communities. As women tend to be active in local government, that development threatens both their public and social roles. Practically all institutional avenues for women's public activity have been closed.

Various women's organizations, that are becoming more numerous and better organized, openly oppose such neo-conservative politics. The plurality of those organizations make it possible to counter-attack in a variety of ways to ensure the preservation of existing rights and to achieve new ones. Their activities consist mainly of promoting constitutional, economic, social and political changes that should improve the status of women. Of particular importance are attempts by some independent women's organizations and some political parties to introduce quotas for women for the leading positions in political parties, to incorporate the "female question" into party programmes, to establish separate female limits for future elections, to preserve local government and participation of women in decision-making, and to preserve the right to abortion and the availability of contraceptives.

It is not possible to predict the outcome of the conflict between the neo-conservative authorities and the women's organizations together with some opposition political parties, but their most important goal is to safeguard those women's rights that are guaranteed by Yugoslavia under the letter and spirit of the Convention.

2/ "Danas", Zagreb, 9 March 1991.

Annex

CONCLUSIONS AND RECOMMENDATIONS OF
THE REGIONAL SEMINAR ON THE IMPACT OF ECONOMIC
AND POLITICAL REFORM ON THE STATUS OF WOMEN
IN EASTERN EUROPE AND THE USSR:
THE ROLE OF NATIONAL MACHINERY
held in Vienna, 8-12 April 1991

A. Economic reforms: women in the economy

Conclusions

1. Economic equality between men and women was recognized as an important dimension of gender equality as well as an important premise for all human rights and national economic development. Equality in principle is not equality in practice. If women are to progress it is necessary to overcome a history of disadvantage.

2. To ensure that women did not bear a disproportionate share of the burden of the social and economic restructuring and to achieve democracy for all, women as well as men, the following recommendations were made for action by government, national machinery, the international community, private institutions and women themselves.

Recommendations

3. Women's interests should be integrated into social and economic policy, including the formulation of structural adjustment policies, by increasing gender awareness throughout government, by ensuring that gender issues are incorporated into all decisions relating to economic transformation and by increasing women's participation in economic decision-making.

4. The United Nations should assist at the national level with regard to public education on the reporting on the implementation of the Convention on the Elimination of All Forms of Discrimination against Women as that is an important international document for achieving equality between men and women.

5. Governments should ensure that social and economic policies are in compliance with international instruments such as the Convention and the relevant ILO conventions, and that appropriate and effective mechanisms are established to monitor the impact of these on women.

6. Positive action (or affirmative action) should be taken to ensure that women and men start from the same point and together progress to equal outcomes. Positive action could include special laws to prohibit discrimination against women, provision of resources, special training or facilities for women to enable them to gain new knowledge and skills and the setting of targets to improve the percentages of women employed and participating in political representative bodies. Positive action should be taken at all levels: in national institutions, local governments, state enterprises, private business and voluntary organizations.

7. All countries of the region should pay increased attention to the application of ILO Convention No. 100 on Equal Remuneration and of ILO Convention No. 111 on Discrimination in Employment and Occupation, as well as of all other international labour statements ensuring equal treatment of men and women workers.

8. The earnings gap between men and women had been significant. Targets for the advancement of women to posts at managerial levels should be set in different sectors of the national economies. Education and training in assertiveness, skill upgrading and career orientation should be developed in connection with the establishment of targets for women in the economy. A system of periodic reports concerning statistical data on the participation of women in decision-making in the economy should be established and made public in order to monitor the achievement of those targets.

9. Educational programmes, aimed at eliminating gender stereotypes and encouraging the equitable sharing of household duties and family responsibilities should be developed at all levels of education, through revision of textbooks and adaptation of teaching methods. Education policies should provide women with a wide range of skills to meet demands of the labour market, and women should be encouraged to plan their careers to take advantage of new opportunities in non-traditional employment.

10. Training and retraining strategies to integrate women into the mainstream economy should apply to employer-provided training, as well as to government-sponsored training. Specifically, women need to be guaranteed access to, and encouraged to partici-

pate in, all forms of training, including in-plant training programmes and vocational, apprenticeship and technical/managerial training schemes. Training and retraining should also be provided to unemployed women and women workers facing redundancy in Eastern European countries and in the USSR. Combinations of entities, including private firms, unions, Governments, women's associations, non-governmental organizations and privately financed skill-training centres could be formed to provide financing and administrative and substantive support for training. Training for women should emphasize and focus upon core transferable skills that can be utilized across multiple economic sectors (both industrial and non-industrial). In particular, specialized attention should be given to the specific needs of urban and rural women in this regard.

11. Assistance should be provided to help countries in the region to establish the type of training infrastructure that best meets the needs of those to be trained in each country and to meet the conditions of each country's economic market. For maximum effectiveness and impact as a tool for eliminating or reducing unemployment, retraining programmes need to begin well before the actual time of lay-off. Retraining should be integrated into a package of assistance that may include, among other services, skill-aptitude testing, career counselling, socio-psychological counselling for coping with unemployment (both individual and family), job search assistance, self-esteem counselling, assistance in household finance (especially for families accustomed to two incomes) and actual financial benefits or assistance. As women are likely to be dealing with both their own job loss and the impact of unemployment on the family, they should receive priority consideration for available retraining assistance.

12. Retraining should be combined with such assistance as the following:

   (a) Child care at reasonable cost, and other supportive services, including transportation, necessary for women to take advantage of training opportunities;

   (b) Placement assistance at the end of the training to ensure a job where the new skills can be effectively applied;

   (c) Social/psychological counselling in how to apply the newly learned skills in a new enterprise/employment environment;

   (d) Assistance to the new employer on where to place the retrained employees to use their newly acquired skills.

13. Employers should provide full pensions, if unemployment is unavoidable. Certain groups of women workers needed special attention, for example, older women faced with early retirement, and younger women. Special training with built-in guarantees of employment and appropriate conditions in the new position could be considered.

14. Specialized counselling services and training should be provided to enhance women's potential as entrepreneurs, given that small and micro-scale businesses, both in urban and rural areas, could offer income-generating opportunities for women. Women should have equal access with men to facilities for such training and consideration should be given to establishing similar facilities specifically for women.

15. Financial schemes, such as revolving loan funds, should be introduced for micro- and small-scale women entrepreneurs. Multi- and bilateral assistance from Governments, as well as from private and non-governmental and international sources should be encouraged to provide the resources needed to support women's entrepreneurship and to train trainers. Special measures are needed in the reform of the banking systems to ensure access to credit and other financial services by small businesses, private farming and liberal professions.

16. UNIDO and ILO should assist in organizing meetings for Eastern European countries and the USSR. In particular, the UNIDO system of consultations should be fully utilized.

17. Public and private investment should be made in social support services in order to remove constraints on women's participation in paid labour activity, in particular child-care services, and family-planning programmes. Women should benefit fully from social safety net provisions, particularly from income maintenance systems (minimum social income, as well as unemployment benefits and minimum wage), which should be gender sensitive and take into account the basic needs of women workers on an equal basis with those of men.

18. Parental leave policies should be developed that take into account the family responsibilities of workers and the reproductive role of women workers. The policies should include paternity as well as maternity leave and benefits. Both parents should have a legal guarantee of return to their jobs after parental leave. Steps should be taken to increase the incentives for fathers to share with child-care, for example, by dividing parental leave time between parents, provision for adequate financial compensation, in addition to the continuation of pension scheme during the leave and by educating fathers in child-care.

19. Part-time and other flexible working arrangements should be available for all workers, both men and women, during the process of restructuring in Eastern Europe and the USSR. National labour

legislation should provide full social protection for all part-time workers.

20. Awareness should be raised to the existence of sexual harassment in the working place and mechanisms formulated to deal with the situation.

21. The collection of quantitative and qualitative data should be improved and gender-disaggregated statistical indicators should be developed to provide better understanding and measurement of the changing economic activities of women and men, as well as family activities, during the process of socio-eco-nomic restructuring. Selection and definition of comparable appropriate indicators should be agreed upon world-wide. Gender disaggregated data and indicators should be part of the standard data collection systems in each country. A series of seminars should be organized in the region that will draw upon the experience of international organizations such as the United Nations Statistical Office, International Research and Training Institute for the Advancement of Women (INSTRAW), United Nations Educational, Scientific and Cultural Organization (UNESCO) and ILO.

B. The role and tasks of national machinery for the advancement of women

Conclusions

22. The meeting noted that, although there were differences between various countries of the region, there were also many similarities characterizing the period of transition and current reforms, which had had serious impact on the situation of women. Those major reforms and transformations aimed at the creation of democratic and pluralistic societies had led to an examination of practically all spheres of public life and its institutions, including national machinery for monitoring and improving the status of women. The urgent need to protect women from the negative impact of the current changes, on the one hand, and to enhance women's opportunities that the process of restructuring offered, on the other, had brought the issue of national machinery and its functions to the fore.

23. Although all countries of the region had, in the past, organizations and institutions dealing with women's issues, those organizations were often established "from the top" with the intention of incorporating women's issues into existing socio-political systems rather than of promoting the genuine interests of women. Those women's organizations were not, in the opinion of the participants, generally considered as national machinery as defined by the Seminar on National Machinery for Monitoring and Improving the Status of Women, held at Vienna in 1987.

24. It was emphasized that no uniform structure of national machinery could be applied. The most effective and appropriate organizational form for an individual country, could be decided upon in accordance with the Forward-looking Strategies for the Advancement of Women, the recommendations of the Committee on the Elimination of Discrimination against Women, and other relevant international standards bearing in mind the concerns and interests of women in the country.

25. Traditional attitudes and prejudices of both men and women were identified as the main obstacles hindering participation of women at the decision-making level. The previous systems had discouraged participation at those levels.

Recommendations

26. In order to ensure the appropriate impact on decision-making process in all sectors, national machinery should be placed at the highest possible governmental level. Focal points for women could be established in all ministries and in units at the regional and local level.

27. Although it was recognized that in order to have political influence national machinery had to be situated at the governmental level, it was feared that such machinery would be influenced by the state authorities and not responsive to non-governmental, grass-root organizations and individual women. Continuous exchange of information on current women's issues between national machinery and non-governmental women's movements should be ensured.

28. National machinery should pay full attention to grass root activities and organizations and to developing linkages with women's organizations, local trade unions, lobby groups, researchers and teachers, so that the concerns of women are reflected in the formulation and implementation of policies

29. Participants recognized the need for both national machinery and autonomous women's organizations to have access to adequate financial resources in order to carry out their activities fully and to employ qualified staff. Exchange of experience with national machinery and international Non-governmental organizations in other countries could be particularly helpful in this regard.

30. It was stressed that both, short-term and long-term goals of national machinery should be given due attention. Implementation of short-term objectives should be closely supervised and assessed. Flexible

response to emerging problems should be encouraged but not at the expense of long-term objectives.

31. As possible priorities for the national machinery at this stage of transition:

    (a) Policies related to women should be developed and their implementation be monitored;

    (b) Gender-specific research and centres for women's studies should be developed, supported and coordinated;

    (c) Information on women's issues and policy content should be exchanged between different governmental structures and between governmental and non-governmental groups;

    (d) Gender-disaggregated statistics should be regularly collected and published;

    (e) Programmes oriented to the advancement of women should be promoted;

    (f) Obstacles preventing women from having equal opportunities with men should be identified;

    (g) Social awareness of women's rights and potential by both men and women should be increased;

    (h) Participation of women in decision-making processes, both inside and outside public administra-tion, should be increased.

32. More information on international legal standards and instruments, as well as United Nations activities and information material in the field of the advancement of women should be accessible to national machinery and that that material should be broadly disseminated within the countries and used for training purposes.

33. An initiative should be made to establish a network within Eastern Europe to exchange information on informal groups and activities.

34. Attention should be given to the development of a legal framework to ensure equal opportunities between men and women, including appropriate legal measures and advisory services to redress prevailing discriminatory practices.

35. The importance of increased participation of women in all decision-making processes was emphasized. Experience could be gained from countries with high level of participation of women in political life, such as the Nordic countries. Various forms of affirmative action and targets aimed at increased participation should be considered. The importance of women's active involvement at all levels of social and political activities was crucial for proper articulation of women's interests and elaboration of women's political agenda.

C. Reproductive rights

Conclusions

36. The Meeting recalled the relevant paragraphs of the Forward-Looking Strategies, particularly paragraphs 150, 156, 157, 158 and 159, and the Convention on the Elimination of All Forms of Discrimination against Women, which has been ratified or acceded to by most of the States participating in the Seminar, in particular article 12, para. 1, and article 16, para. 1 (e). The Meeting reaffirmed the fundamental human right of women to control their own fertility and to decide freely and responsibly on the number and spacing of their children.

Recommendations

37. Governments, appropriate organizations and agencies at the international, regional and national levels, as well as non-governmental and grass-roots organizations should provide necessary information, education and counselling on family planning. Reliable contraceptive methods should be easily available to avoid unwanted pregnancies without having to resort to abortion, and legal and medically sound methods for termination of pregnancy should be accessible.

38. Governments, non-governmental organizations and grass-roots organizations should facilitate the provision and distribution of modern and safe methods of contraception that were easily and continuously available and should provide family-planning programmes and services to all persons, regardless of their social or economic status.

39. Bilateral assistance and support should be encouraged for networking among women themselves as well as among women's organizations to promote, defend and maintain women's reproductive rights, including abortion.

40. Reports of States parties submitted under article 18 of the Convention on the Elimination of All Forms of Discrimination against Women should include information on the national family planning programmes and on the incidence of abortion, and should provide related statistical data.

D. International cooperation

Conclusions

41. For all international cooperation, national machinery has a special responsibility for ensuring that all programmes and projects, regardless of the sector, should recognize women's roles and that women should participate and benefit from the cooperation. The fact that most sources of international cooperation have a mandate to provide particular attention to women, either as part of mainstream activities or as projects targeted to women should be used as an incentive to Governments to take advantage of the possibilities for development cooperation that exist. That cooperation could, variously, be provided by the United Nations system, bilateral and multilateral governmental sources, internationally-oriented non-governmental organizations and by the international private sector.

42. Women's concerns can only be integrated into international cooperation if the national machinery is at a level and in a location that is high enough to give it access to the work of the Government and of the international organizations and agencies concerned. It can, however, be effective only if it is free to mobilize support from grass-roots organizations. For that, it is necessary to provide opportunities and means for the genuine expression of grass-root concerns and their articulation in the policy-making and programming process. The credibility of the national machinery is dependent on its ability to show the importance of taking women's concerns into account in over-all policy and planning.

Recommendations

43. National machinery should establish mechanisms and processes that would permit it to assess whether gender is being taken into account in programmes and projects, and should seek access, formally or informally, to the national ministries formulating programmes and projects. Those should include obtaining information, that could be disseminated to those interested in women's advancement, whether within the Government, in non-governmental organizations, at the grass-roots level or in the private sector. It should also involve the establishment of focal points within government ministries that plan and execute international assistance in order to exchange information and promote the incorporation of women's concerns in programme and project requests by the Government.

44. Efforts should be made as part of international cooperation to provide the opportunity to exchange experiences internationally on different approaches to the organization and functioning of national machinery and in the development of strong interaction between national machinery and women's organizations. That should include activities within the United Nations system, through bilateral cooperation, through exchanges promoted by non-governmental organizations and through private initiatives.

45. International cooperation, technical and financial, should be directed toward priority programmes and projects that are particularly important during this transitional period without losing sight of the long-term goals. Those should include:

(a) Support to national and regional in-depth research on gender-issues to provide a thorough and rapid diagnosis of the situation of women that will permit establishment of strategies and priorities;

(b) Formulation of these national strategies and priorities for integrating women fully into the economic and political restructuring process, including policy-making;

(c) Development of specific projects targeted at key issues related to the incorporation of women's concerns, such as:

(i) Inclusion of gender-disaggregated data in the current reforms of the statistical systems of Eastern Europe;

(ii) Training of trainers in areas such as management and entrepreneurship directed toward women;

(iii) Design of support services for women specifically affected by the reform process;

(iv) Methods of analysis of the potential gender impact of specific approaches such as export-processing zones;

(v) Special research on the monitoring of the impact of reform on women by national institutions;

(d) Organization of regional, subregional and national training workshops on project formulation related to women's concerns for government officials and non-governmental organizations, with the purpose of developing this capacity in each country.

46. In terms of the United Nations system, especially the Centre for Social Development and Humanitarian Affairs (CSDHA), Economic Commission for Europe (ECE), International Labour Organisation (ILO), International Research and Training Institute for the Advancement of Women (INSTRAW), United Nations Development Programme (UNDP), United

Nations Educational, Scientific and Cultural Organization (UNESCO) and United Nations Industrial Development Organization (UNIDO) as well as the World Bank, the resources available to promote incorporation of women in the programming and implementation of assistance, should be utilized fully. That should include:

(a) For the UNDP country programming process, both at national and regional level, participation by national machinery for the advancement of women and provision of technical assistance from relevant organizations of the United Nations system with expertise in the integration of women in development and resources for this purpose should be mobilized and earmarked;

(b) The ECE should take the lead in organizing a regional programme of cooperation by the system to the countries of Eastern Europe and the USSR, including the scheduling of follow-up seminars on specific technical subjects;

(c) Each relevant organization of the United Nations system should review its programmes to identify areas in which they could contribute technical and financial assistance.

47. All bilateral assistance programmes to Eastern Europe and the USSR should be designed to ensure that women participate in and benefit from such assistance. Both donor and recipient Governments should advocate this integration in their bilateral negotiations.

48. Steps should be taken to include national and international non-governmental organizations concerned with women's issues in the planning for and implementation of programmes and projects for international cooperation.

49. Specific efforts should be made, especially by national machinery and by organizations responsible for the coordination of development assistance, to obtain and disseminate information on possible sources of international cooperation at both government and non-governmental levels, including:

(a) UNDP annual development cooperation reporting at the national level should highlight efforts planned and underway that address women's concerns;

(b) An appropriate international organization should prepare and disseminate annually information on possible sources of development cooperation related to women.